OPENING UP

a communication workbook for male couples

Opening Up: A Communication Workbook for Male Couples

Copyright © 2025 by Richard Miller

Published by Pamet Publishing
PO Box 1187
Truro, MA 02666

ISBN 979-8-9926210-0-6
eISBN 979-8-9926210-1-3

Cover design by Mark Pate

OPENING UP

a communication workbook for male couples

Rick Miller, LICSW

Opening Up is a clear, quick-reading, nuts-and-bolts, and, above all, useful guide specifically for gay couples written by a highly experienced gay couples therapist. Ranging from guidance as specific as how to take a breath and get a grip to as broad as the impact of homophobic culture, Rick Miller offers warm, seasoned wisdom.

—**Terrence Real,** *bestselling author; founder, Relational Life Institute*

This workbook is exactly what gay male couples need, and helpful for anyone who works with them. Written by a gay male therapist for gay men, the book is full of education, action tips, and guided meditation. I will ensure I keep extra copies on my shelf to hand out to family, friends, and clients.

—**Tammy Nelson PhD,** author, *Open Monogamy: A Guide to Co-Creating Your Ideal Relationship Agreement*

Opening Up is a groundbreaking, much-needed resource for male couples seeking deeper, more meaningful connections. Rick Miller understands the unique relational dynamics of gay partnerships and provides insightful, practical exercises that foster trust, communication, and intimacy. With warmth and wisdom, this workbook offers a compassionate guide for men who want to strengthen their bond and create a thriving, resilient relationship. An essential tool for any couple looking to navigate love with clarity and confidence.

—**Stan Tatkin** author, *Wired for Love*

Rick Miller's *Opening Up: A Communication Workbook for Male Couples* is an absolute game-changer! Rich with insightful guidance and transformative exercises, this workbook speaks directly to the unique challenges faced by male couples. With years of expertise, research, and real-world experience, Rick has crafted a tool that not only helps couples identify and address issues in their relationships but also fosters deeper connection and understanding.

Gone are the days of guessing what's wrong—this workbook provides a roadmap to navigate those tricky moments and find solutions in a way that's both fun and profound. Each exercise is designed to be simple yet powerful, helping couples uncover the root causes of their struggles while deepening their emotional bond.

For therapists, this workbook is a true gift. It streamlines the therapeutic process, offering practical tools and exercises that can be immediately applied in sessions. Its approach is flexible, making it easy for therapists to adapt to a variety of couple dynamics, including hetero couples, ensuring its broad relevance.

Whether you're a couple looking to improve your relationship or a therapist seeking an effective, evidence-based tool, Rick Miller's workbook is an invaluable resource. I highly recommend it for any male couple, and I'll be using it in my own practice for both male and hetero couples. It's the ultimate guide to fostering healthy, thriving relationships.

—**Lilian Borges,** PLCC, co-presenter *Modern Couples* podcast

*for Oren, my lifelong partner, thank you for pushing me
to appreciate the importance of good communication*

CONTENTS

AUTHOR'S NOTE   xi

Introduction   1

    Living with each other   2

    Living in the world   4

    What this workbook delivers   4

    How we'll get there   6

Men & Resources   15

    A paucity of resources   16

    Our understanding of masculinity   17

    Who does what?   18

    Masculinity   20

    Role Models   23

Your Families of Origin   33

    We reflect what we learn   33

    Destructive patterns   35

    Healing and moving on as a couple   36

    What makes you unique   36

    Where the gay fits in   37

Old Wounds Living in Your Body   51

    The joys of staying calm   52

    Growing up gay   53

    When you know you're different...   53

    Was this actually traumatic?   54

    Relationship ramifications   56

    Constraint   56

    A quick experiential moment   57

    Why self-regulation is beneficial   58

Subculture & Success   73

    Finding your community   73

    Community emphasis   74

Community and couplehood 75

Mandates versus preferences 76

Disappearing gayborhoods 76

Friends and chosen family 77

Double minorities 78

The importance of role models 78

Friendships 80

Sharing your friends 80

Women as friends 81

Friendships with or without benefits 81

The joys (and otherwise) of friendship 82

Why your relationship needs to be supported 82

Sexuality & Intimacy **93**

Sex vs intimacy 94

So... what is intimacy? 95

Pornography 96

You have to be perfect 97

Should the door be open? 98

Finding what works for you 100

Monogamy for gay men 100

Accepting and communicating preferences 101

Developing intimacy rituals, enjoying sex for sex 101

Money and Finances **119**

Challenges of two men melding lives 119

Separate or together? 121

Answering the hard questions 122

Loss of power is the metaphor 123

Avoidance of talking about finances 124

Cultural or family differences 124

But gay men are rich, right? 125

Making purchases 126

What happens when there's a problem? 126

Do what works for you 127

Conclusion   137

NEXT STEPS: What Rick Recommends   147

ABOUT THE AUTHOR   148

ACKNOWLEDGEMENTS   149

AUTHOR'S NOTE

This workbook is intended to be used for informational purposes only. It is not a substitute for mental health treatment. The content reflects the author's perspectives and experiences, but should not be interpreted as medical, psychological, or therapeutic advice.

If you are experiencing emotional distress, mental health challenges, please seek guidance from a mental health professional. The author and publisher disclaim any liability arising from the use or misuse of the information presented in this book.

Introduction

If you're part of a male couple, you've probably noticed there isn't a lot of material out there that pertains specifically to you. Welcome to my world! That's why I wrote this workbook—because there isn't anything else like it.

Why?

Growing up, men aren't taught how to connect with each other. Women are socialized for communication and connection in ways we've never been, and as adult men we need to learn how to get better at this. That handicap—if I may call it that—is why gay men tend to want to do things together. Instead of talking about connection, we get our connection through the activities in which we engage.

This isn't accidental: our own community can be geared toward hook-ups and fun, without paying attention to long-term couplehood.

Many gay couples feel pressured to continue living the way gay men in the scene live... without taking the time to identify how this scene might affect them. Some couples and individuals in couples feel isolated and lonely because certain gay male friends can feel like a threat to their couplehood.

Furthermore, our world is still to some extent governed by the understanding that heteronormative roles dictate relationship norms, and should you decide to go to couples therapy, most mental-health practitioners have little or no experience with gay couples. LGBTQ+ hate crimes are on the rise; micro-aggressions and aggressive acts continue; the current political climate is hurtful; intersectional couples experience even more complicated challenges.

How do you navigate all that?

Male couplehood comes without a training manual, and most of us grew up in heteronormative households. The couples that make it to my office—and I recognize that getting here is no small thing—are the couples willing to find the truth, to take on admittedly difficult work in order to make their life together more connected and more satisfying.

LIVING WITH EACH OTHER

Having said that, it's also true that in some ways it's easier being a gay couple: both people were raised with similar attitudes, and learned similar communication styles as males, which now make sense to each other. And this is an asset when you work at understanding each other, or go to therapy.

But limitations continue to challenge us: we're not part of the majority, and as gay couples we struggle frequently to identify just how we ought to move through the world together, let alone understand each other! There's a certain clarity that's present in heterosexual relationships we just don't have as a baseline; for them, expectations and roles are understood, whereas for us, there's confusion about who does what. How does a couple decide how to take care of things? How do we nurture each other emotionally when we never learned how to be nurturing? How do we talk about vulnerability if we were never taught how to be vulnerable?

Being a male couple can be tricky. There are so many issues that have to be talked about, understood, decided, revisited... issues around acceptance by the community/family, life choices and styles (everything from how to make the bed to whether to have children), work-related pressures, and much more. None of it is going to go away, and the healthiest thing you can do for yourselves, both as individuals and as a couple, is to acknowledge and articulate these common challenges as well as those unique to your relationship, and figure out how you want to deal with them.

The truth is that gay men's relationships take different courses from heterosexual ones. I've been working with male couples for four decades, and have found that unique approaches are important to enabling this unique population to find satisfaction, peace, and contentment in our relationships.

There's a specific challenge for men around being vulnerably expressive with one another. Being independent and strong comes so much more easily to us than acknowledging what might be viewed as "softer" emotions; our culture supports strength in men and belittles deep internal vulnerability or insecurity.

Because men can be less intimate and more dismissive (whether as individuals or as part of a couple), there is also the increased prevalence of intimate-partner abuse, emotional neglect, or even violence because of associated feelings of shame. In addition, male couples experience and cope with societal prejudice in various ways, but the effect of "minority stress," the effect of living with often negative social conditions, always exists to some extent.

LIVING IN THE WORLD

Many gay men struggle with being visible in a world that is not primarily gay, both when they were single and now as part of a couple. Once we commit to each other, we tend to get more involved in the outside world: buying property, having families, sending kids to schools in hetero-normative communities, and all of that presents additional challenges and pressures. How do we choose to adapt to these circumstances? What does that adaptation do to our couplehood? How do we find the balance? What do we choose to reveal—or not reveal—about our lives?

This lack of experience and role models is compounded by the internalized shame carried by most gay men. There's a tremendous challenge in growing up while hiding feelings of love and sexuality—and knowing those feelings are unacceptable (and even dangerous) in the larger culture. Gay men face disapproval, or worse, if those emotions are visible.

Male couples face some of the same challenges as heterosexual couples around issues that include finances and money, sex, chores, children, extended families, work, and recreation, but the specifics as well as the way these issues affect them and how they work them out together can be very different. In addition, issues around physical appearance and politics are considerably more important for male couples, and can provide additional pressures in their relationships.

WHAT THIS WORKBOOK DELIVERS

The truth is that there's very little information that's specific to gay male couples—and even less written by a gay man. This workbook tries to remedy that. I'm a therapist working with gay couples for over 40 years, and I'm bringing my own experiences and observations, including case studies, of the myriad gay men I've worked with. Plus, I myself have been in a long-term relationship for over 30 years and understand the struggles.

So I've created a workbook that:

- **defines issues specific to gay men**

- **provides ideas, tips, and exercises to improve your relationship while speaking to you as a gay man who is understood and supported.**

- **specifically supports a specific kind of couple.**

I'm offering you an appreciation of where and how you live as a gay couple, creating an opportunity to enhance/improve your relationship by providing individual exercises to understand yourselves and take some moments for self-inventory, honesty, self-reflection. The workbook also offers communication exercises tailor-made for male couples to encourage you to grow in your ability to speak to each other about topics you may have felt safer avoiding in the past.

What I hope is that the energy of this workbook will motivate you to a greater sense of hope, confidence, and optimism in the strengths of your relationship and in your lives.

Each chapter presents some theoretical information pertaining to the topic and includes exercises for you to do both together and individually so you can try out some skills you might not have considered before. I'm also giving you the opportunity—through reflections—to think about where you stand/how you feel based on each topic in the chapter. Guided meditations pertaining specifically to each chapter can be done privately or together, and links are included for you to listen to the meditations; and many people experience a deeper experience when they listen rather than read. And, finally, each chapter includes simple tips for improving communication and/or tips for healthier resolution about these topics.

This isn't a replacement for therapy; it's a tool in your overall relationship toolkit. If you're thinking about starting therapy, the workbook will give you some insights to take with you to your sessions. If you're already in therapy, it will help you make space outside of that endeavor to enhance your communication skills.

None of us comes to being part of a couple without bringing our pasts along. How you were raised will play out in your relationship. This book will help you integrate your individual and collective pasts with your present and how you think about your future. Let's face it: most of us grew up in a way that wasn't healthy—hiding who we were, being bullied because of it. We didn't have a whole lot of role models showing us what a healthy gay relationship looks like.

HOW WE'LL GET THERE

This workbook is one tool you can use to address some of these issues together. The exercises here can help you attain that close and comfortable relationship you know can be yours, but just haven't yet figured out how.

Each chapter includes:

- **Information about issues and struggles we all encounter**
- **Guided meditations to help you land inside of yourself for growth, comfort, greater awareness, and sensory connection.**
- **Tips**
- **Discussion points and questions for you to share with your partner, or to write about on your own.**

Are you ready? Then let's get started!

DISCUSSION POINTS AND QUESTIONS TO SHARE

Each of you can take a turn sharing your responses to the discussion points below and appreciate how honesty and vulnerability will help you grow together. You may also choose to write out your answers—whatever works best for you.

Describe your reaction to starting this journey together and what you hope to accomplish. How and why did you end up here today?

_____

_____

_____

_____

_____

_____

_____

_____

_____

_____

_____

_____

Define how you would like to show up differently moving forward.

_____

_____

_____

_____

_____

_____

_____

Share how you already are beginning to feel different and excited due to intentionally agreeing to communicate with each other more.

_____

_____

_____

_____

_____

_____

_____

 **TODAY'S TIPS**

- Approach working on yourself and yourselves with optimism and possibility.

- Affirm to yourself that during this process you will be honest with yourself about what you would like to work on internally in order to help your relationship.

- Commit to being explorative and communicative with your partner.

- Commit to listening to your partner with patience and interest

- Practice and ultimately get into the habit of breaking away from criticizing your partner or telling him what he needs to do.

Let's Start With You

This meditation will help you get ready to embrace discovery and positively explore possibilities of change. As you begin to approach your communication needs and concerns, it's easy to get tense and wonder if you're "doing it right." This meditation will help you relax and welcome this positive step in your relationship.

If you'd like to listen to Rick guiding you through this meditation, either alone or together, scan the code here:

Welcome. Allow yourself to sit comfortably, so that your body can settle into this moment.

You can breathe deeply and comfortably, noticing that with each moment you are feeling calmer and more comfortable. Excellent.

Appreciate how it feels to be here in this moment, and that with each breath, you are able to become more and more relaxed, and even more centered.

Notice how inside your body you are feeling comfortable, and as you continue to breathe deeply, being attentive to your body after reading this introductory chapter, you appreciate all that you are experiencing in this moment.

You're allowing yourself the challenges and the joys of doing something new for yourself, something good for your relationship. This new work will enable you to go deeper, experience your own power and your partners power in the best of ways, and will help you grow, stretch, and change. That is right!

You have known for a while what you've been struggling with, whether it be within yourself or with each other. And maybe you've discussed it with your partner, or perhaps maybe not...that is okay. Because now it is time to be honest with yourself and honest with each other. Excellent. Just take this moment to absorb this inside of yourself.

You are giving yourself this opportunity to face some of the challenges that you've been aware of, and to do it with each other in order in order to get to a better place. You are choosing to live life more harmoniously instead of avoiding the struggles that you have been aware of for a while.

So, begin with yourself. As you are here, now, breathing and feeling comfortable, be honest with yourself. What do you anticipate? And what do you hope for? Starting with you, that is right!

Before you focus on your partner, just think about yourself in this moment.

What do you know that you would like to work on because it will help you in your relationship?

How can you push yourself and stretch yourself to do things just a little bit differently from this point moving forward?

And how do you anticipate this will create changes for the two of you? Excellent.

Think of a moment, or a memory where the two of you were feeling unified and in love, free from conflict, together, alone and happy. That is right! Appreciate what you notice in your body as you remember this earlier time. Allow yourself to connect with this joy and to have the confidence to allow yourself experience joy all over again. Good.

(take space and time with this)

Now, think of a moment where you felt uncertain about how things would go, or maybe entered a tense situation with your partner. You were able to veer away from it and you got on track again. Yes. In this moment, you used your skills, or your honesty to shift gears. Excellent.

Now, allow yourself to feel a sense of anticipation and excitement that you are here, starting a new journey. And this journey will help you to open up, to grow, to open up even more with each other, and just this, in and of itself, will create positive changes. That's right. It is and can be simple. Just take this in.

Enjoy the feeling of knowing that you can do more to make your relationship better, both as an individual, and as a couple. And these efforts will pay off and make a difference. Excellent. You can enjoy the experiencing the feeling of hope once again.

In a moment, you can prepare to bring yourself back to the outside world, feeling the anticipation and encouragement to take on this new journey for you, as well as the two of you. Just imagine what the room will look like once you open your eyes, and slowly reorient yourself to awake and alert. Welcome back!

CHAPTER 1

Men & Resources

One of the most difficult things for gay men is establishing and maintaining trust and connection in our relationships. So to start, let me ask you a few questions...

Do you sometimes feel you're at a standoff in your relationship—you "know" you're right, and he "knows" he's right? Have you found it difficult to agree on a compromise, or even just find some common ground? Is being right more important than getting along well and respecting each other's needs?

If this sounds at all familiar, then you've come to the right place to find alternative ways of being together! We're starting things, as we saw in the introduction, at something of a disadvantage, since male couples have few if any role models, and the couples' literature available may not fully fit your particular needs as a gay couple.

A PAUCITY OF RESOURCES

Most gay couples have few community resources. Communities that are part of your day-to-day life may not be familiar with the nuances of gay couples. It's also probable that you've been careful in terms of the breadth and depth of the information you've shared with your families. Even friends aren't necessarily helpful, as their advice may come from a different model of being a couple. Specifics about your relationship, experiences as gay men, or norms of the gay subculture are details you prefer to keep private about.

In addition—and it's sad to need to say this—there are few long-term gay couples to serve us as role models. Previous generations may not have survived due to the AIDS epidemic; additionally, men have been trained to not discuss intimate or emotional matters with each other. In other words, even if you're gay, you learned how to be a man from people who aren't. Now it's time to explore and celebrate what unique and beautiful attributes partners in a male relationship bring to themselves and to each other.

And there are role models out there, even if you don't know them personally. This workbook features case studies involving several gay couples, to give you an honest vision of how others have survived and dealt with the struggles you're experiencing.

These challenges may include:

- **feeling isolated and alone in your experience**
- **knowing you look better to others on the outside while feeling something is missing**
- **finding connections difficult**
- **fitting into gay life even when it doesn't feel like the real you**

OUR UNDERSTANDING OF MASCULINITY

My practice encompasses a significant number of couples who come to me because they have no blueprint—for being gay men, much less for being a gay couple.

So I'll begin by telling you what I tell them: You are a real man. We have to start with that: no matter what your childhood, your family, or your community may have implied—or told you straight out—you are a real man.

That said, you've probably grown up feeling somehow "different." Because you grew up feeling disenfranchised/flawed, you disowned the masculine energy inside yourself. As you come to terms with your awareness of being a man, you will experience amazing personal growth. Modes of masculinity may not be what you buy into—but how you're viewed is going to be from that perspective.

Male relationships can run into challenges from the start, because two men coexisting as men don't necessarily know how it works. It's not intuitive. Some men have internalized homophobic assessments of masculinity and so may be uncomfortable with their partners' expression of what could be perceived as femininity. They live in a world in which they had to be hyper-masculine and have trouble tolerating anything else in their partner because of how those traits reflect on them.

Depending on your culture, your partner's being perceived as gay may very much matter to you, and obviously can be a major source of tension. Establishing comfort within both you and your identity as a couple can help—and finally create how you carry yourself in the world as a couple.

As we look at the paucity of resources, another consideration is generational.

I myself remember that when I was a young man, older gay couples scared the hell out of me: they seemed prissy, fussy, and frankly stereotypical. I didn't see myself that way, but didn't have any other role models, anyone who could show me a different way of being part of a couple.

Years later I was facilitating an intergenerational group with men from twenty-six into their late seventies. Hearing the experiences of these older men turned out to be so beneficial for young gay men who may not understand the magnitude of the challenges prior generations faced!

WHO DOES WHAT?

There's a wonderful scene in the movie *Pride*. A male couple is in conversation with a straight woman. "So," she says, "you live together as man and wife? So, what I want to know, is..."

One of the men nods and says, "I know what you're going to say."

She continues, "...which of you does the housework?"

He takes a moment. "Okay," he admits, "that isn't what I thought you were going to say."

But it's a reasonable question. Although straight couples are—rightly— challenging gender roles within marriages and relationships, they do at least have a starting-point, an accepted norm. We don't have that. So we're floundering around, trying to navigate everything from tenderness to chores to caregiving to receiving love. How do we ask for what we need? How can we respond to our partner's needs? How do I show up for him? How can I make myself vulnerable?

Male couples have the flexibility of deciding how they want to live rather than accepting heterosexual norms of what a relationship should look like. That is a little scary, for sure... but when you think about it, isn't it liberating? You can decide what works for you. There's a lot of power in that.

So many factors come into play with male couples, but one I'd like to high-light in particular is competition. We're socialized from the cradle to be competitive. This gets reflected in nearly every facet of our lives: open relationships, social experiences, career and financial achievements, a sense of respect in the world, betting, sports, overachievement... the list is endless.

There's no blueprint, and the opportunities for competition are also endless given that role of masculinity is a propeller in people's lives whether they know it or not. How many of us have heard, "you're not enough of a man"? That's the negative unconscious energy living inside every one of us, and if we only had a plethora of different kinds of role models we might be a lot closer to self-acceptance and self-actualization.

DISCUSSION POINTS AND QUESTIONS TO SHARE

Each of you can take a turn sharing your responses to the discussion points below and appreciate how honesty and vulnerability will help you grow together. You may also choose to write out your answers—whatever works best for you.

Masculinity

What is your own definition of masculinity as an individual?

_____

_____

_____

_____

_____

_____

_____

_____

Do you meet this definition of masculinity within yourself?

_____

_____

_____

_____

How do you perceive yourself of falling short of masculine?

_____

_____

_____

_____

_____

_____

_____

Do you worry about being recognized as an individual or a couple who looks gay or appears effeminate?

_____

_____

_____

_____

_____

_____

What measures do you take to conceal or hide this from others? (Family or communities that you are part of?)

_____

_____

_____

_____

_____

_____

_____

Describe if you have ever felt self-conscious about your partners open expression of being gay.

_____

_____

_____

_____

_____

_____

_____

Role Models

Who are the influential couples that have been in your life?

_____

_____

_____

_____

_____

_____

Are they public figures or private friends or family members?

_____

_____

_____

Are there gay couples who have been together for a long time that you admire? If so, in what ways?

_____

_____

_____

_____

_____

Are there long term couples who aren't gay that you admire? If so, what are the qualities of that relationship that you admire?

_____

_____

_____

_____

_____

_____

_____

Describe what qualities from couples who you admire that you would like to emulate in yourself and in your relationship?

_____

_____

_____

_____

_____

_____

_____

# TODAY'S TIPS

- Some say that masculinity is a construct and that there is no true definition of masculinity. Whether or not you agree with this, think about how the construct of masculinity pressures you and allow yourself to be who you truly are rather than how you should be.

- You probably felt different from the regular guy while growing up, or the stereotypical guy now that you are an adult- appreciate that you have been raised as a male and how much this has actually shaped you.

- Accept how you have actually reached a place in your adulthood where you can work harder at expressing your authentic self.

- Allow yourselves as a couple to be less concerned about appearing a certain way on the outside, and while being out in the world, simply be the couple as you are. You will appreciate how accepting and welcoming others are of your couple hood.

- Experiment with being a little more daring and little less stereotypically masculine in order to recognize that things can be less fraught than you realize.

Owning Your Masculinity

This meditation will help you explore how you feel about yourself as a man, a person, a partner. It's meant to help you relax as you realize how valued and valuable you are as an individual.

If you'd like to listen to Rick guiding you through this meditation, either alone or together, scan the code here:

Begin by getting comfortable in the seat or the couch in which you're sitting.

Just take a few easy, deep breaths, and as you exhale, recognize how it feels to breathe away tightness and tension that you've been holding in your body throughout the day.

Appreciate how much tension exists inside without your even realizing it. Instead, enjoy these few moments of comfort, of peace and quiet, excellent. You've got this! Settle down into this zone of comfort and relaxation.

Really appreciate what it feels like to be inside your very own body in this moment.

There's absolutely nothing to do, nothing to hide, nothing to conceal you are here in your own private space with the goal of focusing on yourself and being exactly fine as who you are.

Even though you may have struggled throughout your childhood or even into your adulthood with trying to be the person other people wanted, you get to be you in this moment. You get to simply focus on being who you are- and who you are is good enough, and you get to enjoy how good it feels to be you.

So take this moment for yourself, just for yourself, only yourself and trust that it is just perfect, excellent.

It may take a little bit of work, but you get to like yourself for who you are, and this is a big accomplishment. Nice job. And now take a moment and go a little bit further and allow yourself to imagine what the word man or masculine means to you. Notice any shifts or changes inside of your body,

appreciate what just happened...

Did you tense up?

Did you shift positions, or did you allow yourself to stay in this comfortable zone of pleasure when you thought about masculine?

You probably had some words that popped into your mind or some images that came to you. No doubt you probably felt a bit insecure, or felt as though you fall short of this ideal that we define as masculine.

Now, go back to yourself, back to the comfort that you were aware of when you started this meditation and you went inside. Take the time that you need to return to the relaxed state that you were in before. Good job.

Appreciate that even though some tension came into your body, you are perfectly able to redirect yourself back to comfort, back to the space within yourself that is just perfect. Excellent.

Again, you've got this! Take time to enjoy the breath, to allow your belly to remain soft and to have your body be free of tension.

Explore the ways in which you truly are your own version of masculine, all your own. That's right.

Rather than being the man society expects you to be, simply be the man that you are. There isn't a right way. There isn't a wrong way.

The benefits of being gay are that we have wiggle room to allow ourselves to be outside of the box. And the true meaning of masculinity is being strong and the way in which you can be strong is to be yourself. That is all. You can and will be less concerned with how you are viewed by others, and from this point on you will feel more grounded in the expression of your own self and your own masculinity. Yes, this freedom is now yours in your own authentic way, and as you appreciate this, allow The feelings of comfort to become bigger and larger inside.

Each breath is slow, rhythmic, really powerful and really good.

Being a real man is being exactly who you are. You don't need to constrict yourself. You certainly don't need to hide yourself and instead you get to be and express the authentic person that you truly are, excellent!

Perhaps you've been noticing the ways in which your body has been shifting and tensing up during these prompts. Just breathe away the tension. Rearrange your body into comfort again and again, as often as you need. Breathe even deeper in this moment until you notice comfort that continues to expand itself in your lungs, in your belly and your entire body, excellent.

The true man inside of you is the true person that you are. It is that simple! Continue to enjoy this moment, appreciate how you are doing right now.

Notice how you may have been struggling during this mediation, while also allowing yourself to take the time that you need, both now and when you finish doing this,

to understand where your barriers about masculinity exist-where they come from, and how you will push yourself to grow and expand beyond your fears in order to be the person that you truly are. This person, this self, this man, comes from within, it is you. That's right, your strength comes from within yourself. Excellent.

And now take a moment and think about your relationship.

How is it that you may have wished your partner would change in the way that he expresses himself in the outside world, to not call as much attention to himself, or conversely, how is it that you may wish your partner would let go just a little bit more expressive and not worry about how he comes across to others.

How is it that the two of you together can simply be and you can worry less about how you come across and how you will be perceived? Worry less about whether you are good enough, strong enough or manly enough- and instead enjoy the presence of who you are as a couple. Appreciate the magic that shows how the two of you make a wonderful couple. Appreciates this and how no modifications need to be made. You are who you are, and you two are perfect just as you are.

Picture yourself looking at some photos of the two of you together. These may be photos that you actually have, or photos that you create in your mind. The two of you are happy together, look like a perfect couple together, and appear not to have a care in the world. Notice how you feel inside, as you look closely at this beautiful photo.

And as you share this photo with others, you get continual affirmation with those that you share it with. Notice who is commenting, and what it is that they say about you two.

Now you can look at other photos of you two together. You are the perfect couple, a male couple who looks good and are perfectly suited for each other. That is right.

When you are ready, imagine what it will be like when you bring yourself back into your space. Slowly begin to re-orient yourself by wiggling your toes or fingers, taking your time to bring yourself back. Just bring yourself back gently, slowly, opening your eyes, coming back, and feeling good. Excellent.

CHAPTER 2

Your Families of Origin

Every couple has the task of integrating two very different childhood and adolescent experiences when they join together. This isn't unique to gay men. We all bring a set of beliefs, fears, norms, habits, and experiences to the table, and navigating a new, third set of norms that will support your life together is neither easy nor immediate.

WE REFLECT WHAT WE LEARN

Our families, and in particular our parents, taught us what we know about relationships and intimacy. If one parent was distant, we come to expect distance or ward against this distance through escalating needs. If one parent's needs or desires were constantly frustrated, that too becomes a relational expectation with others. If a family accepts and respects every member—well, that's a great way to grow up, and it could put you on better footing when negotiating boundaries in your own relationship, yet this can be rare.

Many of you have heard this old adage: when you go to bed with your partner at night, there are actually six people in bed together, each of you—and both sets of parents! But the truth is there are many more than six: ancestors, community members, other influential family members join you as well... so make room!

Your family of origin naturally has tremendous impact both on who you are today and on how you interact in your current relationship. Through the lens of your family, you have viewed and learned how the world operates, and who you are as a person, based on their behavior, feedback to you about the world, themselves, or you as an individual.

You also learned, both directly and indirectly, how love, pain, communication, disappointments and joy are experienced and communicated and coped with inside the family system. Somewhere early on in working with all new clients—not just couples—I ask people to describe what home like was like when they were younger, and inevitably this opens up Pandora's box of events and memories. How can it not?

Despite how adept gay men are in remaking their lives, they can't shed themselves or deny the truth of how their backgrounds formed them. Even if you were raised in a healthy environment, in a functional, intact family, you'll still experience pain and disappointments—especially if you are gay.

But the result of living in a healthy home environment imparts innate tools and a sense of how to fit into a family (or, in your case, couple) system. You know how to connect and love others, how to cope with disappointment and communicate about it, and can take inventory of your flaws and choose to work on them for the wellbeing of your relationship.

This all sounds nice, doesn't it? Yet even healthy people struggle in relationships and have work to do to disentangle from recurrent dynamics that create tension in your couplehood.

DESTRUCTIVE PATTERNS

There are individuals who grew up in inconsistent homes for any variety of reasons—a change in circumstances, financial shifts, parents' separation or divorce, a traumatic event that shaped your overall childhood, a parent's substance abuse or other addiction, or personality traits of either of your parents that alternated between loving/communicative or unavailable/angry/punishing.

This kind of inconsistency in family life can create great confusion, and learning to navigate the inconsistencies in the system is both exhausting and confusing.

People who grew up with inconsistency have the challenge of learning how to trust the reliability of others, of allowing themselves to trust their partners, and of knowing that their relationship can help them heal from the dynamics of their family of origin. But it's a slow and detailed process that frequently takes years to do. Understanding and being able to describe this background and process to a partner who also understands and is invested in shifting the dynamic for you is both an important and a daunting task, and it can't be done alone. Ideally, a partner will understand why it is important to be perceived as reliable and trusting, even if he knows that he already is.

The other type of negative family experience involves blatant ongoing trauma or cruelty. Unfortunately, people born into impoverished communities, adopted under traumatic circumstances, removed from the home due to parents' inabilities to provide healthy parenting, or ongoing abuse, are much more likely to have difficulties forming healthy attachments later in life. If you're one of these people, then the lack of safety in the world may have made it easy to move along in your life and find better circumstances for yourself, but most likely there are some old shadows remaining that impact how you allow yourself to be loved, to love or nurture your partner, and to trust that you actually are a desirable and lovable man. The challenge of remaining present given these circumstances can be daunting, but it isn't impossible. Resiliency and determination to create a better life are far more attainable than you might think. And you deserve to be one of the people who makes this happen.

Our past experiences of the world can make us vulnerable to responding in old, outdated, and not useful ways to present experiences. We all feel this. Cherish and protect the vulnerability in your partner.

HEALING AND MOVING ON AS A COUPLE

What all this means is that being in your relationship is not only challenging based on the day-to-day stressors that create issues between you, but also that these significant factors in your individual histories need to be processed, shared, and understood by both partners, and that your relationship needs to provide the safety and healing from your experiences in your families of origin.

It's time to get to know each other more deeply. As scary as this sounds, this is how you will become closer to each other.

The point here is that our emotional reactions and communication patterns are initially learned through the families in which we grew up. While gay men may reject their families of origin due to traumas or lack of acceptance regarding their being gay, they can't just disown these families, because we all bring them with us, even if it's unconsciously. We embody them inside of ourselves, and a part of them lives with us, impacting how we think or how we feel inside. Sometimes we may sense some unanswered questions gnawing at us, and it's more helpful to make sense of these questions rather than ignoring them.

WHAT MAKES YOU UNIQUE

Individually, our task is to make sense of how our family is a part of us. We have to choose to emulate loyalties, connections, or traditions that we identify with and want to include internally as part of our own identity. And there is also the opportunity to own—rather than disown—where we are from. Owning doesn't mean we need to act like our family members (from whom we're attempting gain distance, after all!), but instead to appreciate and understand how our family has impacted us in painful ways, and to use resilient resources we cultivate to allow ourselves to appreciate who we are in relation to our family while staying free in order to create our own independent identities.

The goal is to be fully independent as an individual in order to be a loyal and available partner. This means you need to see what's getting recreated in your relationship that stirs up unfinished family-of-origin business. Each person in a relationship has challenges based on inevitable tensions with their partners, challenges that stir up issues from our family that may not necessarily be fully resolved. This is the magic (or, for some, the curse) of a relationship—that we get to (and need to) come to terms with what our relationship is stirring up inside about our families, and figure out how to handle those issues in order to be fully present. Rather than recreating an old dynamic that no longer serves us in healthy ways, it is preferable to live in the present with our partner.

WHERE THE GAY FITS IN

Most likely, you grew up in a mostly heterosexual family where heteronormative norms are what you know. So where does being gay factor in?

It's complicated to know what to bring from your family to your present relationship. It's probable the norms of your family don't quite fit, but you are attempting to create your own healthy family with your partner and so some of what you learned from your family can be brought forward with you.

Questions to think about and discuss with your partner

- **How was gayness experienced or dealt with in your family?**

- **Were there conversations or references made to being gay or was it unspoken? Elaborate on the tone in which it was discussed (Or whether it was overlooked).**

- **Was anything about homosexuality articulated?**

- **Where there/are there older gay family members whose presence can serve as a model to your family or even yourselves?**

- **Were gay people respected and treated well by your family, or discriminated against or made fun of?**

Being aware of your background helps you appreciate how your own comfort and discomfort about being a couple is dealt with within your family. For many people, there is some self-consciousness about being out and open with family, so it's easiest to keep secrets and be vague about details of your day-to-day life... but that can feel sad. Breaking that pattern and trying at greater inclusivity is more rewarding, but also involves work.

Finding and connecting with others who have gone through a similar process can be helpful—and offer the kind of support you need. One such organization is the Family Acceptance Project, a research, intervention, education and policy initiative to prevent health and mental health risks and promote well-being for LGBTQ children and youth in the context of their families, cultures and faith communities.

Even though you may resent being in a position to have to fight for your own acceptance within your family, it's a worthwhile endeavor. Families can and do come around with exposure and education about LGBTQ issues, and may eventually accept their gay siblings and children warmly. It is worthwhile for you to push for this, especially in the light of what it will mean for you and your partner.

Any rituals you each bring to your relationship should be honored; expanding your repertoire as a couple to embrace both backgrounds—including food choices and recipes, holidays, games, and more—will not just enrich you both but can also create additional listening opportunities. The same goes for sharing cultures, religions, and ethnic heritages, and what all these things mean for each person. You'll want to discuss which holiday rituals can/should be shared, and which feel more personal. Is it okay to do a hybrid approach based on histories, or should each person have his own turn?

Remember this: there is no guidebook for living as a gay couple, no right or wrong ways to do it, so you have the freedom to decide what works best for you. Remember that it's okay to include some parts of your past and reject other parts... as long as you do it carefully and thoughtfully.

Though living away from your family may provide escape or relief, you still bring them with you, deep inside. Within the gay community it seems easy to be able to remake our lives into something that fits into expectations of the worlds where we live now, but we should also recognize and own within ourselves where we have come from.

DISCUSSION POINTS AND QUESTIONS TO SHARE

Each of you can take a turn sharing your responses to the discussion points below and appreciate how honesty and vulnerability will help you grow together. You may also choose to write out your answers—whatever works best for you.

What did learn about relationships from my family of origin?

_____

_____

_____

_____

_____

_____

How did I choose to live similarly or differently in my own partnership as a result of growing up in my family?

_____

_____

_____

_____

_____

_____

What lessons am I grateful for learning (whether they be through joy or through pain)?

_____

_____

_____

_____

_____

_____

_____

_____

What family dynamics have I vowed not to recreate in my intimate relationship?

_____

_____

_____

_____

_____

_____

_____

What characteristics from my family of origin do I notice getting played out in my relationship?

_____

_____

_____

_____

_____

_____

_____

How will I work more purposefully to change these patterns?

_____

_____

_____

_____

_____

_____

_____

_____

How can each of us continue exploring our families' influence on each of us in a way that feels authentic?

_____

_____

_____

_____

_____

What lessons or insights might help me show up differently? Even while embracing my own family traits?

_____

_____

_____

_____

What lessons or insights might help me show up differently? Even while embracing my own family traits?

_____

_____

_____

_____

TODAY'S TIPS

- Honestly assess how your family of origin has shaped you.

- Spend more time on regularly exploring it instead of tucking it away.

- Own rather than minimize what you have embodied from family dynamics including aspects of being gay.

- Maintaining loyalties with your family's idiosyncrasies keeps you from developing your authentic self.

- Freedom and differentiation from our families come from allowing ourselves to be who we are.

Guided Meditation
Your Family of Origin

This meditation will help you explore the dynamics of your families of origin, and how they influence your current relationship. It will help you recognize and understand the impact of your family's behaviors and lessons on your own lives, including communication styles and attitudes toward being gay. All this will help you with self-awareness, acceptance, and the choice to either embrace or distance yourselves from these family traits now. We'll conclude with a return to the present, emphasizing the importance of being authentic and fostering a fulfilling relationship with your partner.

If you'd like to listen to Rick guiding you through this meditation, either alone or together, scan the code here:

Take a moment and settle in comfortably as you are seated or lying down. Just begin by taking in a series of deep, easy breaths. That's right.

As you breathe in, allow yourself to settle into comfort and as you exhale, Just exaggerate the "out" breath in order to breathe away uncertainties or tensions. Excellent.

Notice where you feel tightness or tension inside, and as you continue to sit and breathe comfortably, appreciate the ways in which you settle in. Focus on comfort more than anything else. That's right.

And now prepare to take a journey back in time. Go back to being a child. You can choose the age that feels right for you. Imagine looking at some old photographs of you and your family, or being on a trip with them somewhere. Or if you prefer, you can bring yourself back to your childhood home, where you grew up.

Look around, and see who's there. Notice what you see, think, or feel in this moment. You are getting closer to being with your family back then. And as you identify a point in time, notice how old you are and what do you look like back then? What is your hair like? What are you wearing? What were your favorite toys or things that you liked to do most back then? Really take your time revisiting this place.

You are fully immersed in the memories of your own childhood, and as you think about your family of origin, this may include extended family as well, or just your nuclear family. You're currently aware of sensations and feelings inside your body, because your family provided you with the blueprint of how to be in the world as well as how to be inside of yourself. This blueprint also forms how to be in relationships with others as well. For some people, these family dynamics are comfortable and joyous, whereas for others, these family dynamics are painful and challenging. There is no way that you should feel or be. This is simply an opportunity to explore your family and the impact they have had on you.

In this moment, you're receptive to the realities of what you were taught from your family, and some of these lessons may have been

direct lessons where you were told how to be and how not to be in the
world, where some of these lessons may be indirect, may have been
indirect where you recognized that there was a norm in your family
of how to do things and whether this was good for you or not good
for you. It's what you knew, and these particular family dynamics
were the ways in which your family was different from anyone else.
Again, for some, these are good dynamics. For others, painful from
your family. This is where you learned how to be, how to feel, how to
express yourself, or how to remain quiet.

As you're sitting here now, you're identifying the unique characteris-
tics that are part of your family, part of you. You don't need to do or
change anything, just recognize what's coming to you. You can now
move forward in time to your adult self, focusing on the feeling of
being present in this moment, with your eyes closed, doing this guided
meditation. As you think about your current partnership, you realize
and own what you bring from your childhood into your relationship.

Maybe you vowed that you wouldn't repeat some of these patterns,
but you do, and that's okay. Or maybe you simply hoped that certain
aspects of communication that were once part of your life wouldn't be
replicated in the present. Perhaps they do now, and that's okay as well.
It's good that you're able to recognize any of these traits.

Aspects of your being gay may also include how your family, how
your family dealt with being gay back then, how your family discussed
homosexuality, or dealt with gay relatives, whether it was spoken
about, avoided, ignored or welcomed. Appreciate that all of this is
what you bring with you, into the present, and that your family's

experiences have shaped you, whether you've tried to escape them or simply enjoy bringing them with you.

In your current intimate relationship with your partner, your family is with you, you've embodied who they are, along with who you in this moment.

You can spend even more time identifying the ways in which you continue to be like them. Choose to identify the ways in which you are both like them, and different from them. It's perfectly fine to allow yourself to do this, because now you are a fully separate adult compared to how you were as a younger child. You are your own person, your own individual, and you get to be who you want to be, and it feels good. Excellent.

As you sit here being the person that you want to be, make space inside of yourself for this reality and enjoy how it feels to have given yourself permission to be yourself in your own real, authentic way. That's right.

This moment will stay with you. Perhaps it'll be a turning point of freedom, of individuality, of contentment.

And as you think about your relationship with your partner, you can make it a point to show up differently. This can be inside or outside. You will be able to push yourself a little bit more, by being more expressive, by sharing what you are experiencing inside of yourself in your own unique way. Rather than doing it the way that your family has taught you, you get to do it in your own way now, and that feels really good.

You've made this shift and you will continue to be aware of this as you live your life and continue along in your relationship.

Each day and every night you will identify with your family in the ways that you choose to, and will also distance yourself from family traits should you no longer need in the present. You now embrace your relationship with your partner even deeper, that is right. Both you and he are the family where each of you lives now. This family is yours, place that you choose to be in, with each other. A home that brings you satisfaction. A home where you welcome in elements and people from your family of origin, yet also a home where you welcome new rituals and ways of being that are uniquely yours. Your past and your present can merge together and you enjoy being where you are at this very moment in time. Excellent. You are home.

Now, when you feel ready, and you've received exactly what you've needed from this exercise, slowly prepare to bring yourself back to the outside world again. Just wiggle your toes, wiggle your fingers, slowly, reorient yourself and bring yourself back to the outside world, feeling present, feeling good, alert, and opening your eyes. Welcome back!

CHAPTER 3

Old Wounds Living in Your Body

One of the biggest challenges of being in any relationship includes maintaining calm in the midst of feeling a shift or threat. One doesn't need to have a trauma history to feel this. Over time we come to know and expect certain reactions from our partner, and then we react, internally first, then outwardly. This is the normal ebb and flow of an interpersonal connection.

The challenge is to maintain clam before reacting, in order to not overreact. Overreactions are a cause of unresolved tensions in a relationship. It is easy to assume you know what your partner is doing or about to say. It is also common to misinterpret what is happening between the two of you and jump into defensive or self-preservation mode before deciphering what is true.

The more we can maintain calm, the more apt we are to prevent a misinterpretation from turning into a full-fledged argument. This happens in two ways, by keeping ourselves calm and steady in how we react and take in things, and by keeping clam and steady in the ways that we speak to our partners.

We all carry the weight of our past experiences with us, and they inform our current selves and relationships. If you have been through a traumatic experience, you may find that it has changed you in many ways, including affecting your partner and your relationship.

Living through previously painful events may result in expectations of danger or potential harm within new or old relationships. Survivors may feel vulnerable and confused about what is safe, and therefore it may be difficult to trust others, even someone you love. It may feel frightening to get close to people for fear of being hurt in an unsafe world. Or people may feel angry at their helplessness and the loss of control in their lives, and become aggressive or try to control others.

THE JOYS OF STAYING CALM

A "therapy" expression for this is "self-regulation," the ability to understand and manage your behavior and your reactions to feelings and things happening around you. It includes being able to regulate reactions to strong emotions like frustration, excitement, anger and embarrassment; to calm down after something exciting or upsetting; to focus on a task and refocus attention on a new task; to control impulses; and to behave in ways that help you get along with other people.

Self-regulation is essential to trauma therapy, for virtually all survivors deal with ongoing emotional reactions to things that remind them of the past (triggers and secondary alerts) and with the increased vulnerability to stress that usually follows trauma.

The joy of self-regulation is in allowing us to be more resilient and bounce back from failure while also staying calm under pressure. Therapists and research has found that self-regulation skills are tied to a range of positive health outcomes. This includes better resilience to stress, increased happiness, and better overall well-being.

GROWING UP GAY

When people have experienced significant—or even mild—trauma in their past, many people adapt by living life in a scattered or non-regulated state. During trauma, your brain adapts to protect itself from the stress trauma produces. Certain parts of the brain are placed on high alert, while other parts become much less active. The body enters in to protection mode and may shut down.

Since childhood, many gay men have adapted a stance that is self-protective and doesn't necessarily include being regulated in a healthy way. Being regulated means being in control, behaving consistently and having self-control in order to get along well with others, particularly your partner.

Chances are that the majority of you reading this have been made fun of or bullied while you were growing up. Most gay boys were mocked by their peers, even long before they knew they were gay or came out. If these kids weren't bullied and called "faggot" or "sissy," perhaps their experience with being gay would could have been easier.

WHEN YOU KNOW YOU'RE DIFFERENT...

Long before being aware of what gay even meant, many boys knew they were different. This is practically the universal experience for gay boys growing up. Societal and community standards pretty much dictated how boys were supposed to act, and what activities were okay (or even more clearly not okay) for them to do.

Not fitting into a narrow mold of expected behaviors provokes both fear and shame. Many of my gay clients have shared the great lengths they went to in order to get by under the radar, not get "found out," and slip by in school in order to not be noticed or bullied.

Easier said than done. For many boys, interests that were typically more "girl" than "boy" couldn't be squelched. Loving Barbie dolls, cooking or sewing, or style, while possessing absolutely no interest in sports sets them apart. Many gay boys hung out more with girls than with boys—and were consequently made fun of.

Secrecy, shame, fear, and the sense of not being good enough are experiences embedded inside their bodies. Boys who weren't white and grew up in a predominately white world found the danger even more pronounced.

Though grown men are able to talk comfortably about their pain growing up, and frequently make light of it, many forget just how painful it was going through childhood and adolescence. Compartmentalization was a tool that "worked" for them, otherwise pain fear or trauma would have ruled everything. But if it works in the short term, it can cause damage over years and even decades.

Additionally, family members frequently know that you are different. There are all kinds of arrangements with this-challenge, confront or humiliate, ignore and push out of sight, or simply not address it while you knew and or they knew what the truth was. These are the more painful experiences, and it wasn't always this hard for everybody.

WAS THIS ACTUALLY TRAUMATIC?

People make a lot of assumptions about trauma. Trauma is a pervasive problem. It results from exposure to an incident or series of events that are emotionally disturbing or life-threatening with lasting adverse effects on the individual's functioning and mental, physical, social, emotional, and/or spiritual well-being.

In particular, many people equate trauma with sexual abuse, and while that abuse is clearly traumatic, there are many other ways of experiencing trauma, and we disregard them at the peril of our wellbeing.

What is trauma? It's all the negative and disturbing things you feel after a disturbing experience or event: fear, helplessness, confusion, and so on.

We can be over-eager to use the term trauma to define various occurrences in our lives. Once we define them as trauma, we can be held back by not understanding all the various experiences and attitudes that have been traumatic to us.

Whether you fall under the precise definition of trauma or not, as a gay man, you most likely have endured more pain than did many other children growing up, and this constant fear and worry of being found out, exposed or bullied has shaped you. You don't automatically shed your coping mechanisms—learning to keep things quiet, being secretive—when you become an adult. These mechanisms may have helped you cope at the time, but they may hold you back once you enter adulthood. Hundreds of clients I have worked with over the years have habitually restrained themselves and kept many aspects of daily life secretive even though it is no longer necessary.

Many gay men have been raised in communities and families where being gay is considered a sin. Conservative religious communities teach this. Others who were raised in less religious families also experienced homophobia from various family members and learned to protect themselves by pulling away, or misrepresenting themselves with others. This takes a toll.

If you have grown up living your life like this, even if you experiences are less intense than what I have just described, you have created a "false self" in order to get by in the world. What is the toll this has taken on you? When you think about living in a world where you have been secretive or hidden, you can appreciate that confinement has been the usual stance inside of your body. Not only have you outwardly protected yourself through pulling away, but internally, you have protected yourself with a palpable stance of constriction. Now, with some work, you can work on expansion, comfort and visibility.

RELATIONSHIP RAMIFICATIONS

If you've read this far, then you're probably realizing that two men who grew up being held back, and diminishing the essence of their true selves, may easily continue to unintentionally carry out this dynamic between themselves. Male couples can easily be brittle, distant, and uncommunicative. Sex can be hot early on, and your commitment can be solid, but learning to talk to each other about what you experience inside emotionally, physically, or even on a deep somatic level is something that will add to the pleasure and intimacy or your relationship-yet you have probably lacked training in how to do this.

I frequently notice in couples' therapy that clients who are willing to take risks in session actually begin speaking on a deeper level than ever before. Of course, it doesn't come quickly or easily. It may take weeks of encouraging and pursuing on my end to get individuals in the couple to reveal what they actually are experiencing in a given moment—even though they are actually in no danger from their partner. Even when nothing historical or old is getting played out, old habits can be hard to release.

CONSTRAINT

The goal here is to break free from constraint and allow each of you to grow in comfort and spontaneity with each other.

Constraint may be a concept with which you are all too familiar, perhaps without even recognizing what's happening. Growing up and not fitting in, and being ridiculed, doesn't come without a price. Part of the price you pay for this is holding these memories inside of your body. The body keeps the score is a popular concept defined by Bessel Van Der Kolk in the trauma field these days: somatic memory is stored in the body.

I repeatedly see how my gay male clients hold themselves: rigid in posture, and clenching their cheeks, neck, or shoulder, hunched over and self-contained.

It takes two men in your relationship to be open and more free from constraint. This is how success is achieved-with intimacy, and in solidarity with each other. This is the ultimate goal!

If either or both of you continue to struggle with being contained or unexpressive, or holding in your own experiences of pain in your lives, then the growth of your relationship will be compromised, even when it doesn't need to be.

This isn't easy. Working on this may result in your needing more than just having this workbook. Seeing a therapist who has experience in working with trauma and has expertise in working with gay men may be great choice for you!

The goal in your relationship is to allow the relationship to help release you and allow yourself to heal from old pain. This brings possibility into your lives. The possibility with living in greater ease and connection. If you tend to these individual needs within each of yourselves, you have the opportunity to live happily and with more freedom.

As I have said, hiding can be a habitual reaction to growing up gay. If you don't shed this in your relationship, you may continue to live life as two men traumatized, when in fact your relationship may be the factor that allows each of you to grow from being with each other. The strength of your mutual bond will help make what wasn't okay then, okay now. Sharing more with your partner can bring to wonderful places together.

A QUICK EXPERIENTIAL MOMENT

A quick experiential exercise is below. It calls on simple skills that you hopefully have mastered many times before, whether you are aware of it or not. This includes being able to modulate yourself by breathing deeply and rhythmically, while noticing how your body begins to respond, and them realizing that after a few moments, you've become more and more calm. I'm asking you to do a clenching and letting go, to accentuate the relief in feeling calm.

Tightening your body and letting go

Take a moment and imagine this clenched posture I just described. Appreciate that this posture of being rigid comes from being contained, the opposite of being or feeling free.

As your eyes are closed, assume this posture for a moment and exaggerate tightness and tension by clenching your body as hard as you can and hold it, just for a few moments.

Notice what happens as you exaggerate this stance.

Now, let go and exhale. Instead of constricting your posture, hold up your neck and shoulders, releasing tightness in your entire body, and feel the relief.

Notice how different you feel in this moment!

You have just created shift within your body, a somatic shift that enables you to approach life from a proactive, and energetic approach.

The somatic experience reminds you of what you have endured throughout your life and what you can release yourself from in a moment's notice. I frequently ask clients to do this throughout the day to recognize how constricted they may feel throughout the day without realizing it. The letting go is an easy reminder that you can shift how you cope on a somatic level by embracing softness and release.

WHY SELF-REGULATION IS BENEFICIAL

Everybody with a history of pain or trauma benefit from developing self-regulation skills as an individual. However, it is also important for couples' success as well.

Self-regulation for individuals:

- **You will benefit from developing a reference point that is different from what you have internalized all these years. You will maintain a new way of being in control.**

- You will break the cycle of feeling like an underdog and instead become strong and confident.

- The somatic success of being strong and regulated will enable you to bear more emotional challenges.

- You will have a feeling of being in control. You will understand what is happening inside of yourself when you are feeling threatened, and you will be able to find your way to comfort inside.

- Being reactive without losing your temper or jumping to conclusions means you have control over how you are doing and how you are feeling.

DISCUSSION POINTS AND QUESTIONS TO SHARE

Each of you can take a turn sharing your responses to the discussion points below and appreciate how honesty and vulnerability will help you grow together. You may also choose to write out your answers—whatever works best for you.

One of the ways that individuals heal is by creating opportunities to be their true selves with others instead of trying to adapt or meld to the expectations of others, which certainly take a tool for boys growing up who are different from others. Doing this with your spouse is even more profound because it builds up intimacy and enables both of you to know each other more, and paly apart in the healing of each other. Bearing witness to your partner's vulnerabilities are a powerful components for healthy attachment.

What were the ways that you experienced pain or mild trauma because your differences in masculinity were exposed?

_____

_____

_____

_____

_____

_____

_____

_____

How did you cope with this internally?

_____

_____

_____

_____

_____

_____

Did you try to cover this up on the outside and how?

_____

_____

_____

_____

_____

_____

Did covering up work?

_____

_____

_____

_____

Were you made fun of or bullied as a child or adolescent?

_____

_____

_____

_____

How did you feel about it? Did you tell anybody about it? And how did you try to minimize or hide it?

_____

_____

_____

_____

_____

As you remember these moments how are you feeling emotionally and what are you noticing inside of your body?

_____

_____

_____

_____

TODAY'S TIPS

- Emotional restraint is a skill that each of you learn to possess, enabling you to get along better and understand each other more.

- You will both be able to endure stressful moments with each other and maintain emotional and physical wellbeing during stressful times.

- You will jointly exist in a confident interpersonal system where both of you will be fully present and engaged with each other.

- You will be able to emotionally nourish each other and benefit from these intimate moments.

- The experience of mutual control will maintain calmness and cooperation with each other which will greatly impact challenging moments. You will simply do better with each other!

Three Ways to Self-Regulation and Calm

This meditation will help you become present to your own body and feelings in the moment, existing in a sense of self-regulation. It will allow you to gently look back and recall times when you were blissfully happy or frightened and confused, and deal with the feelings separate from the experience. Finally it will demonstrate how being part of a couple can be comforting, amplify a sense of safety and security, and help you both feel stronger going forward.

If you'd like to listen to Rick guiding you through this meditation, either alone or together, scan the code here:

Part One: Self Focus

Just focus on breathing. Take a few easy, deep breaths and allow yourself to get comfortable. Excellent.

As you're breathing, just soften your belly, release any tension in your temples, your cheeks, your neck and shoulders, breathing deeply.

In this moment, the only thing that you need to do is to be present right here and right now, excellent.

To help you go even deeper into this zone of comfort, I will count backwards from ten to one. Notice how your comfort increases little by little, with each descending count.

Ten, nine and eight, deeper and deeper into the zone of comfort.

Seven, six and five, deeper and deeper.

Four, three, and two, and finally, one.

Appreciate being in the moment now. As you breathe, you feel more connected to your body, and more grounded.

Breathing is effortless and easy, and you are fully relaxed. Maybe you need a few more moments to just breathe deeply, or to be even more relaxed. Just give yourself this. You can bring yourself to this place. And notice how good it feels. That's right.

In this moment, you are connected to your body, to yourself, to the comfort that you have created through regulating yourself, and all of it is coming from you.

It's as if I have said to you, ready, set, go, except there's nowhere to go in this moment, except be here. Excellent.

This is mindfulness, this is comfort, this is self-regulation. This is the way in which you are able to be in joyous moments or stressful moments, while also maintaining a steady stance for yourself. That's right. And now let's move into the next part.

Part Two: Bodily Sensations

The next part of this meditation is to notice shifts that take place inside of your body as you recall different events.

So, allow your mind to remember a moment of joy. And it may be a moment of joy from a long time ago, or a moment of joy that has taken place recently.

Where was it? When was it? How did it feel?

What were the circumstances and what was happening inside of your body at that time?

As you look back, notice what is happening right now. Are you able to incorporate the contentment that comes with this joy? Are you able to appreciate experiencing this joy actually helps you in this very moment? That's right.

Feel good, feel open, and feel appreciative of what you're capable of achieving for yourself.

You can allow yourself to do this, and it is a good moment.

Now allow yourself to remember a moment of frustration or mild pain.

Just like joy, it may be something that took place long ago, or maybe a few moments ago, or recently.

Notice what changes inside of yourself as you remember this moment, a subtle shift in your breathing may have taken place, or your heartbeat may be a little bit different. Your body may be shifting more and you may feel as though you lost the zone of comfort, but you actually can bring yourself back to that comfort easily, by going back to the depth of each breath, and breathing deeply, being calm, enjoying where you are right now and reminding yourself that you can regulate the subtleties and shifts inside of yourself.

And yes, it takes a little bit of effort, and it may take a little bit of time, that is fine, because you can modulate your own body and bring yourself back to a place where you can become still and quiet. Excellent.

So maybe "ready set go" is simply permission to bring yourself to calm,

Still and quiet. Excellent.

Appreciate that there are various experiences that take place, both inside and outside, and that you can tolerate these variations more than you realized until this very moment.

And part of the reasons that you can endure this is because you can modulate your breath and your being.

Imagine that you have your own ability to speed things up and slow things down as needed, and It feels good to be able to do so. You have this skill all on your own.

Excellent.

You can appreciate that you can handle shifts and changes that take place with a greater sense of calmness and comfort and even though fluctuations happen in life and your body responds to them, you are now in this moment, reminded that you have the tools to tolerate these shifts and maintain a steadiness inside of yourself. This is something that you own. This is your tool, something you can use over and over again.

You feel good because you can remember this and feel it, and you will remember that you can rely on your own self as much as you need to in the future. That's right.

And now we will shift into the third part of this experience.

Part Three: Comfort From Togetherness

Imagine your partner is next to you.

Picture a moment of comfort where the two of you have been or are together. Perhaps there were no words that are being spoken, but it just feels good to be in each other's presence, like settling into a really comfortable space together to watch TV, perhaps on the couch or the bed. It's just warm, cozy and comfortable. It is just a moment of comfort and stillness. Appreciate that being in each other's presence elicits warm cozy feelings.

Notice the feeling of well-being for both of you. Your togetherness intensifies between you two and the safe feeling inside of your body is reassuring and you can enjoy it now. Yes. This is something that you get to enjoy from being with each other, simple casual presence that is easy to have, without even having to try too hard. Excellent.

Or another simple moment of togetherness might be riding in the car together where a song that both of you enjoy is playing, so you turn the volume up and you share the experience in this moment. Simply driving and enjoying the music with each other, without even needing to talk. Good.

It isn't the most powerful moment, it simply a time where it feels good to be sharing lightness, through motion and music. It is nice to be reminded that sometimes being together gives you more than being alone. Simple moments of closeness is what it is all about to feel light and feel good. And this good feeling is something you notice inside of your body. Appreciating the nice feeling, the ways in which your breathing is calm and quiet, and that the overall posture of your body is soft and comfortable.

You appreciate being with your partner can allow comfort to enhance itself, and using these simple tools help you to be mindful and to enjoy the comfort that you create with each other. This really is simple.

And now, just for a moment, bring yourself to a place where you feel a slight tension with each other. Maybe it is spoken, or maybe unspoken. Simply recognize how easily your comfort can shift and change, from pleasure into tension. Even though you might wish to not have to go this place, you also appreciate that this is a normal part of being with your partner. These moments are inevitable. And as you accept this truism, it feels more manageable, less threatening. And you can tolerate shifting from lightness to tension, and from tension back to lightness.

This is how you adapt to being in a healthy relationship. You can do this. You can breathe. You can stay still. You can regain control. Excellent.

This is the place that you go inside to find calm, and instead of reacting or overreacting, you can maintain stillness within yourself, and appreciate that whatever it is that causes tension, is actually manageable, by you.

As you already know, tension can be managed. You can manage your own tension. You have your own ability to modulate, to tolerate this, and find your way of feeling okay again. Good.

Sometimes in a moment of tension, we can bring ourself back to this okay place without even letting our partners know where we have gone or what we are doing. It is perfectly okay to take a moment of quiet, finding calm once again, and then joining him once again, back to that space of comfort!

This is doable. This is how you keep things stable, calm and good.

Now just take a few final moments of peace and quiet as you continue to breathe deeply, you will remember that you can enjoy the moment with just a bit of work. You can be present, you can enable comfort and stability to be yours. Bringing it inside , regardless of what may be happening outside.

This is your strength, these are your tools. The challenge is yours, and you can do it. You are regulated, and you are strong. You bring this skill with you by practicing breathing, being in the company of others and enjoying the ways in that you remain calm, peaceful and fully present.

Excellent.

Notice how you're feeling in this moment. Make a commitment to continue working on this, it's the best gift that you can receive.

Taking a few easy breaths before joining the outside world again. At your own pace and in your own way, bring yourself back to the outside world, opening your eyes, coming back, feeling good, feeling strong, feeling alert and awake. Ready, set, go, fully alert!

CHAPTER 4

Subculture & Success

Perceptions of gay culture have changed dramatically over the last century. Before the Stonewall Riots of 1969, mainstream American society chose to not acknowledge the existence of a gay subculture. After the Stonewall riots and the emergence of the gay liberation movement, the declassification of homosexuality as a psychiatric disorder, the defeat of sodomy laws and, finally, the legalization of gay marriage, there was more freedom to not imitate heterosexual culture and unions and instead find a way of defining gay from within the gay community.

FINDING YOUR COMMUNITY

As gay men, we grew up on the outside, knowing something wasn't "right," that we didn't fit in. Coming out for many of us was a big relief. And an important part of coming out is finding the tribe or group to which you belong.

After feeling alone, different, even sometimes despised for so long, finding that community gives us a sense of coming home. There's finally a place where you belong, a place where you can feel open and free to be yourself, people who are like you. That "place" is both emotional and literal; there are neighborhoods that remain primarily gay, and there are still gay clubs and bars, though fewer than there used to be for a lot of reasons, some of which are encouraging—there's more acceptance out there in the world and we don't have to be confined to gay ghettos anymore. Still, many of us miss those places where everyone was (almost) just like us.

COMMUNITY EMPHASIS

No community is perfect, and in fact some community norms can be damaging. The gay male community follows strict codes about how we should look, where we should live, and how we should live. This comes with high standards that are internalized by men without being questioned as much as they could be.

In my psychotherapy practice I have heard from hundreds and hundreds of clients expressing feeling self-conscious about their appearance. This used to be in comparison to how others looked at the gym, in town, or in the press, but now we have the gift of social media to drive that notion and that comparison home even further. Most people who see muscular, youthful, retouched images of the most beautiful men all over the world assume that this is what most people look like, meaning they don't feel like they make the cut. And this feeling isn't reserved for people who are 10 pounds overweight or are not beautiful, everybody is included here. The most beautiful men have felt this feeling of failure and have the same struggles with accepting themselves.

Feeding into this is the social media frenzy that has gained particular people public figure status. Those lucky enough folks who have the right look and find their way to stardom online end up feeding their followers with constant updates on everything they do—with or without clothes—and onlookers get extra hits of inadequacy without even realizing it's happening. It is a norm of being connected.

COMMUNITY AND COUPLEHOOD

Though this seems relevant to all gay men and not particular to couples, there are added components to being in a gay couple that poses particular challenges.

This includes how you feel about yourself as an individual and your overall sense of worthiness as a partner in comparison to others out there. But it also includes who you select as mate and who you perceive worthy of being your spouse, even if that is just on a physical level. In our hook up culture, we are so accustomed to pursuing perfection and masculinity, that many men overlook potential partners who don't meet their cut for their ideal spouse. This is only accentuated by the apps that are used where continuing to scroll for someone "better" is the template for finding Mr. Right.

There is little awareness of what is important in looking for a suitable partner. Most of the media available to gay men is about looking great, hooking up, and being out there. Much less information and support is available for those pursuing a relationship.

When you pursue a relationship or are in a relationship, chances are that not only will you feel a great sense of excitement and newness, but perhaps some fear or even loneliness.

Other gay men who are "living the life" in the scene are choosing a lifestyle for themselves that may not go in tandem with your goals within a relationship. As a result, it is common for couples to pull away from the scene and their gay community in order to nourish their relationship.

Many clients who I have seen have commented that they feel as though the gay community is unsupportive to them and, for the sake of protection, they don't have gay friends, they find that too threatening.

I am not saying that the gay men out on the scene are solely responsible for this, but that the couples who are busy protecting themselves from the scene are participating in a social pulling-away that doesn't need to be as entrenched as it is. Self-protection can be limiting or lonely sometimes.

MANDATES VERSUS PREFERENCES

An important reminder: we get to choose how we live. There are no mandates, though we forget that. Appreciate how you choose to be in the world. How your couple hood is a creation of mutual preferences along with the communities that you are part of, including cultural, ethnic, work, family, and social.

Nobody is forcing you to make choices to live or be a certain way, but chances are that you need to remind yourself of this-perhaps frequently. The pull of the gay male stereotype of how to be is more powerful than most realize.

Many couples report feeling dull in comparison to the typical gay man out there. They have internalized a pressure and feel insufficient. The challenge for a couple is to simply make choices based on your unique sensibilities and preferences, and feel good about these choices, including wardrobe, furnishings, location of residence and even foods that you eat!

DISAPPEARING GAYBORHOODS

In the old days, most urban centers had a section of town where gay men lived. For a multitude of reasons including acceptance, gay couples are not needing to live in the gay neighborhood anymore, or they have drastically shifted and are now folded into the community at large.

What does this mean to you as a couple? It means that being accepted may be easier, or may be more risky. Living in the gayborhood meant there were many other folks living there just like you. For couples, it may have meant having an easy way to grow a friendship network, and finding other couples nearby who were living similar lifestyles. Plus, they didn't just have to meet each other at bars. Sitting on the stoop was a way of making friends!

As gayborhoods are more diluted now, and more gay couples are leaving the city for the suburbs or the country, there is an added pressure about how to socialize, what to reveal to neighbors, and how we are perceived by others. Some couples feel as though they need to be a little more careful about what they reveal about themselves, and actually revert back to being more [private and protective. One client who lives in an affluent suburb reports seeing all of his neighbors gathering for various events and feels both envious and sad for being left out, especially since his child is the same age as the neighbors.

FRIENDS AND CHOSEN FAMILY

Who you choose as friends for the wellbeing of your couple hood is also important. You want people in your life who support and care about you, both as individuals and as a couple. Should you only choose gay men? Should they be single or in couples? Just men, or other genders? Does it matter?

Obviously, my intent is not to dictate anyone's choice of friends, but what I can say is that having a variety of friends is rewarding and supporting of your couple hood, and these should be the folks that you pursue. The quality of these friendships is more important than any question of gender, sexual orientation, religion, and so on.

That said, the reality is that other gay couples will have a commonality with you that's rewarding on a number of levels. They will have experienced many of the same obstacles and joys that brought you together and that you live out every day. And that can be an added resource: observing and learning how other male couples interact, solve problems, and create a life together can be helpful as you look to do some of these same things in your relationship.

Remaining close with your single friends is also important, and choosing when to participate in activities with these single friends—and when not to—is important, based on your own preferences and the comfort and stability of your relationship. Isolating yourself from others to preserve your relationship may be too extreme, while being involved in the scene without being attentive to the wellbeing and needs of your relationship is just as extreme. Find your preferences and honor them according to your own wellbeing and that of your partner.

The notion of chosen family is a privilege we are fortunate to have. Out of necessity in early days, LGBTQ+ individuals had to find safety amongst people who were accepting of them, and the notion of chosen family emerged.

Hopefully many couples aren't rejected by their actual families, and get to enjoy closeness with both biological and chosen families, but we have the freedom and flexibility to enjoy our friends as our chosen family. Cultural pressure to only be with our families is less rigid and we have the luxury of spending "family time" with our besties.

DOUBLE MINORITIES

Gay men who are Black, Latino, Asian, Pacific Islander, or Native American are members of what we can think of as a "double minority." In other words, it presents all the problems of being part of a minority, but on steroids.

Intersectional individuals and couples have a built-in expectation of rejection, have experienced discrimination on various levels, have a greater perceived need for concealment, and have internalized not just homophobia but also racism.

Members of a double minority can have interpersonal and familial issues as well as intrapsychic conflicts that affect the successful development of an affirmative identity and self-esteem. Don't downplay any of the effects you may be feeling. Especially if only one of you represents a double minority, communication will be key.

THE IMPORTANCE OF ROLE MODELS

It's beneficial to have role models in all facets of life. Instead of embarking upon challenges that we need to figure out all by ourselves, which frequently replicates earlier experiences of not being "out" and feeling alone, there are healthier options. Affiliating with others who have already been there and done that is supportive and relieving.

There are people out in the world, both gay and not gay, who are living a life aspects of which you may want to emulate. We've always had elders in various communities we've used as role models and mentors. It's an incredible source of strength and keeps our stories alive along with showing us how others have walked the paths we now find ourselves on.

Sadly, along with the rest of the elderly, older gay men are frequently tossed aside, invisible even to those of us in their communities. These men have lived through things we haven't and have somehow survived... isn't it logical that they might have a thing or two to teach us? They could be a source of strength and inspiration to us.

Imagine how our relationships could be enlivened and improved through contact with these older men and older couples! Imagine having a sense of a different genealogy, the genealogy of our chosen families instead of just our biological ones! Imagine the stories these chosen uncles and cousins could share that would tell us how we got where we are. They have years of living in the world as a gay man behind them, years of challenges and happiness, of forging a way forward without a roadmap. Why wouldn't we want to use the roadmaps they've worked so hard to provide?

I remember when I was 23 years old and newly out, accompanying my partner to a dinner party hosted by an older male couple. The crystal, the places-settings, the predictable conversational forays, all of it awakened in me a level of self-loathing, all the homophobic slurs I'd ever heard materializing in front of me as they conformed to stereotypical "gay" behavior. I was so limited in those days! Now I wish I could tell that young man how fortunate he was to be in their presence, tell him to look beyond the chatter and the China patterns and ask them questions, appreciate their experiences of life had been as a long-term couple in their community and their families. I could have learned a lot that evening. It's unfortunate that it took me decades to realize that.

Consider that we have a lot of freedom as compared to our forefathers. They had fewer choices around behavior and survival. So it's perhaps a good idea for both individuals and male couples to consider the choices we do have today and make them thoughtfully. There's an unspoken mandate in our community to be out there, sexual, beautiful, and social. If that is the choice you want to make, it's fine. But it's also fine to question it, to see if your couplehood can align with how you want to be in the world as individuals.

FRIENDSHIPS

Many men are in general not great at forming and maintaining friendships, whether they're gay or straight. For most men, friendship centers around activities. Men's purpose is to do the activity; the result is closeness. (For women, the purpose is the closeness, the activities the result.) The notion of initiating a friendship immediately casts the shadow of our fear of vulnerability; so we tend to not do it.

For gay men, the significance of friendships in our growing-up years may have been life-saving, so they take on an aura that nothing in our contemporary lives can touch. As we lose contact with those early friendships, we don't replace them with equally affirming relationships in the present. This is a mistake.

Friendship also gives male couples validation, which can be a profound experience. By and large, heterosexual couples get constant validation from family and society; we don't, or at least not yet. But having a circle of friends that care about you, both as individuals and as a couple, can offer that validation and strengthen your bonds.

SHARING YOUR FRIENDS

When a male couple first connects, each brings "stuff" to the relationship—property, career, family, interests... and friends. In the best of all possible worlds, existing friendships get folded into the relationship, but this takes time and patience to do; there are the inevitable sexual tensions along with friends' possible judgments about the new partner and/or the perceived viability of the relationship.

Most men find it easier to fold in old friends when there's a shared activity involved. If you're all avid tennis players, or like watching old movies, or are taking a painting class together, it gives the opportunity to talk together about the activity before taking the risk of moving into deeper areas.

WOMEN AS FRIENDS

A lot of male couples choose to have women as friends for a number of reasons. There's no sexual tension with a woman, so men feel freer to hang out and talk, have a meal, go shopping, whatever, without the concerns of attraction and possible rejection. Women give us a free pass in that sense.

But on a deeper level, women are more in touch with their feelings and much more inclined to talk about relationships. This is an opportunity for a gay man or a male couple to explore feelings—again, without tension or judgment.

Many gay men exclusively choose the company of other gay men. But for so many reasons, this is cutting yourself off from people who can be substantive friends, offering an intimacy that has nothing to do with sex. In my experience, men willing to risk expanding their circles and allowing women in have been enriched by these connections of love and respect. A good friend is a good friend. Age, circumstances, gender; none of that matters, it's the connection with another human being that is important.

FRIENDSHIPS WITH OR WITHOUT BENEFITS

A lot of gay men form friendships as a result of having initially hooked up together. They continue to flirt with each other as a matter of course; we tend to continue things the way we started them. This can cause tensions when entering and sustaining a relationship.

The norms among gay men around social media are often sexual in nature; we post provocative pictures, our followers (i.e., friends) make provocative posts, and so on. This is usual and few men take offense at it (unlike straight couples—I worked with one partnership in which the wife was horrified and jealous that her husband complimented another woman!).

But there's always an element of tension that exists if your close friends are also men you're attracted to. It can stir up jealousy in your partner and some men just shut down when it happens to protect themselves and their feelings. And it only gets worse if left unaddressed.

THE JOYS (AND OTHERWISE) OF FRIEND-SHIP

We've grown up being made fun of, disenfranchised, protective, and so naturally as adults it's scary and vulnerable to take charge and initiate something that could make us vulnerable. Forming a close-knit group of other gay males is a special experience of chosen family, men who spend holidays together, travel, insulate themselves from the world. The disadvantage to this practice is that you never venture outside that bubble... and you literally never know what you're missing.

Men are positioned to expand outside of the box if they're willing; their pasts have forced them to deal with adversity. Why not continue the benefits of those lessons? Busy-ness in careers, in relationships, homes, all provide a safe excuse to not feel too close to people, which means that many men don't have as many friends as they optimally should have. Especially in couples who aren't part of the scene, there can be loneliness unless they're open to friendships.

WHY YOUR RELATIONSHIP NEEDS TO BE SUPPORTED

The truth is, the gay community doesn't necessarily support aspects of a long-term relationships. The old joke, "Where do gay men go on their second date?" answered by, "What second date?" can be perceptive. Men tend to focus on beauty, variety, and availability. Heterosexual men struggle with this issue, as they are involved with women whose needs and priorities are quite different; but being involved with other men means we're that much more likely to view couplehood, with or without monogamy, as stifling. The fear of missing out runs rampant through our community.

This leads to a number of stereotypes: all gay men cheat, everyone does hookups, apps and clubs are the only places to meet other men... the list is long. And of course a lot of it is true—stereotypes don't become stereotypes without a basis in fact. So when a man chooses to be in a long-term relationship with another man, the community doesn't know how to support them.

And in fact the community can undermine them. Sabotage of others' relationships is an ever-present danger. Many single men are so absorbed in the scene that they don't recognize what it would be like to talk about the scene with a couple that isn't part of it.

Some long-term male couples respond by cutting off ties to the community. They keep to themselves, only see other long-term "safe" couples socially, don't put themselves in positions where they might be tempted or their relationship sabotaged. This is one solution. Others try and work out a middle way between abstaining from contact with the scene and fully engaging in it. My own sense is that success is not buying into gay norms, but being your own couple in the midst of outside pressure. And that can be challenge enough!

DISCUSSION POINTS AND QUESTIONS TO SHARE

Each of you can take a turn sharing your responses to the discussion points below and appreciate how honesty and vulnerability will help you grow together. You may also choose to write out your answers—whatever works best for you.

Make an honest assessment of your closest friends between you and your partner. Appreciate your good fortune for those that you are closest to. Also share what you could do to nourish these relationships.

_____

_____

_____

_____

_____

_____

Assess whether you might be lacking certain connections or friends in your friendship circle and consider what actions you can take to welcome more of these people in your life.

_____

_____

_____

_____

_____

_____

Share with each other about your mutual involvement in the gay community and whether you have enough of this—or too much of it—in your lives.

_____

_____

_____

_____

_____

_____

_____

Who are your role models? Allow yourselves to have older people in your lives who can serve as mentors of sorts. Sometimes it is easier having people who have gone through what you are going through to help support you as a couple. Commit to incorporating these people in.

_____

_____

_____

_____

_____

_____

_____

Prioritize how you as a couple can fold in more of your chosen family with your actual family if this is an option.

_____

_____

_____

_____

_____

_____

_____

_____

_____

_____

_____

_____

_____

_____

TODAY'S TIPS

- Think honestly about lifestyle decisions that you make to fit into norms in the gay community

- Think about how you would like to or could allow yourself to make shifts that are more reflective of you as a person rather than being part of your group.

- Consider the ways in which your life and lifestyle is reflective of you as an individual rather than as a gay man.

- Think about your closest friends and chosen family. How many are gay men, how many are women? How many are younger or older than you? Allow yourself to expand!

- Enjoy the relaxed version of you when you aren't comparing yourself to others in the gay community. (Including your appearance, your home, wardrobe, etc.)

Guided Meditation
Finding Your Community

This meditation guides you to relax deeply, release tension, and connect with your inner self. It emphasizes your ability to create comfort and joy from within, independent of external influences. By reflecting on moments where you made choices purely for yourself, you can remember of the ease and fulfillment that comes from living authentically. The practice encourages you to carry this sense of inner peace and self-guided decision-making into your daily life, shaping your experiences with intention and authenticity.

If you'd like to listen to Rick guiding you through this meditation, either alone or together, scan the code here:

Just take a few moments for yourself. Get comfortable in your seat, uncrossing your legs, allowing your feet to rest on the ground. Your arms are by your side, and you just take in a few deep, easy breaths. Excellent.

Just notice the ways in which each breath coming into your body brings you a sense of comfort and relief, while also noticing that each time a breath leaves your body that you breathe away tightness and tension. Any energy that has created discomfort simply fades away.

Now just enjoy the energy that brings you warmth and wellbeing. Great.

Notice the ways in which your body is settling in. Just a few moments of doing this allows you to feel more comfortable and more centered. Your arms are feeling heavy in a really good way, and your legs are as well. Notice that there's a softness in your belly and your chest as you're letting go of tension in your neck, your head and your shoulders. That's right.

Your whole body is becoming more relaxed, more still, more quiet.

It's really nice to have this experience. Really nice to give yourself just a few moments to settle in and be reminded that inside of yourself is this ability to find comfort, to find joy, to be in a place that is just right for you. Excellent.

As you are enjoying this comfort, appreciate that you are creating an experience inside of yourself, All by yourself. Excellent.

Your frame of reference is coming from within rather than outside.

And you will remember this exact moment for a very long time. This is a time when you created your own sense of contentment. A time where with some effort you've found your way to feeling good, all by yourself.

Instead of relying on outside forces to tell you how to be, or exactly how to feel, you have brought yourself here on your own.

You really are capable of enjoying who you are from within. Great.

Allow yourself to take this experience and plant it as a seed for the future. What you want, what you choose to leave behind is totally up to you. And even more important is that instead of living your life as dictated by the groups you have been involved in, such as your family, neighborhood, or group of friends, you can make personal decisions that simply work best for you. That is right. This is important!

Now allow yourself to go back in time. Go to place in your history where you chose to be exactly where you wanted to be and were doing exactly what you wanted. It may be a distinct moment of simply playing alone as a small child with your favorite toy and being in a blissful moment as you were absorbed by the way that it was the only important thing you were doing at that very moment in time.

Another example might be how you chose to do something really important for you when you were younger, such as choosing a musical instrument, or a place to visit, or even something else that was very important to you in that moment.

You didn't have to work hard to decide what was right for you, you just listened to a desire within yourself and made what you wanted to happen a reality for you. Excellent.

Appreciate how in a memory like this, you were less focused on what "they" (your family or peers) wanted, and instead you were focused on your own desires. What they thought didn't matter nearly as much as what you chose just for yourself.

Appreciate this memory and enjoy the ways in which certainty feels effortless and light.

As you are in this state of awareness, your body feels a lightness and a warmth. Remember this and allow this feeling to be your guide in the future. This is what you will strive for in order to remind yourself that living from the inside out will be an important priority for you. You will always have the ability to choose from this healthy place within and be reminded that your best life, happiest moments and best relationship moments come from you being authentic in your choices. Excellent.

Now simply prepare to bring yourself back to the outside. Remember what you have achieved from doing this, and how you have been reminded that your life is your own to shape and enjoy.

Imagine what the room will look like when you open your eyes in a moment or so, just wiggle your fingers and toes to slowly reorient yourself, coming back gently, opening your eyes, bringing yourself back. Back to the outside world!

CHAPTER 5

Sexuality & Intimacy

With heterosexual couples, male sexuality is markedly different from female sexuality, and these differences can create conflict in heterosexual relationships. So you might think that two men in a relationship, sharing a common sexual framework, would be an ideal and conflict-free couple. Right?

Well... Many men learned about sex in ways that aren't conducive to living in a relationship, and the role models available to gay men are not necessarily healthy, as we've seen earlier in this workbook when we looked at the baggage we bring from our families of origin or what we've understood about the norms of the gay community.

There are a plethora of assumptions and stereotypes relating to gay male sex in general, but certainly most particularly about gay male partnerships, and it's easy to fall into some of those stereotypes in your thinking. We all have an idea of what we want in a partner, but gay culture may be telling us something else— that we have to be frenetically sexually active, that our bodies must be perfect, that we can have everything straight couples have and then some.

There are certainly many different models of being a couple, from monogamy and open relationships to being polyamorous. The essential, I think, is to recognize that there is no wrong way to have a relationship.

SEX VS INTIMACY

Men don't exactly know how to navigate intimacy. Sex is easy; connect intimacy to your sex life and that's where we stumble. There's a split between how we think we're "supposed" to be as gay men and what we're craving in a relationship, and as we've already noted, we're pretty terrible at communicating our feelings around that dichotomy.

The reality is that many of us "met" through sex. Gay men hook up on apps designed for that purpose; sex is the primary bond before there's any intimacy, and as the relationship develops, the expression of caring gets folded in—but with awkwardness. After all, how do you translate something "hot" into something close and caring? Men simply aren't socialized to be intimate and nurturing. And with all the expectations we've heaped onto sex, that's not the best place to develop those skills.

Yet it's what we do because we don't know how to do anything else. Just recently I started seeing a couple who didn't know how to express any kind of intimacy together, so they've been using the bar scene and alcohol to "make things better." Drunken sex may be fun, but it's no route to intimacy.

So... what is the difference between sex and intimacy in your relationship?

It really comes as no surprise that men use sexuality for intimacy purposes. It's close to intimacy, after all: it's physical contact and it passes as intimacy for many. And since you probably grew up silencing your needs for both sex and intimacy, it's a challenge to suddenly accept and grow into those needs with your partner. How do you learn how to nourish the person you love? How do you learn how to ask for what you need from him?

Male couples come to my office being absolutely solid together in frustration and anger, while spending a lot of time avoiding any expression of tenderness and caring. They see the results in everything from day-to-day household conflicts to any attempted expressions of vulnerability.

Many couples find it easier to be sexual over time; many are good at being sexual with each other right away; some want extended intimate foreplay while others want to just dive right in. None of this is wrong, as long as you're on the same page, listening to and communicating with each other. What about developing a repertoire where you're more able to convey your caring and commitment to your partner?

SO... WHAT IS INTIMACY?

There are a lot of ways to define it, but here's some of what I see: connection, understanding, empathy, a desire to please and to take care of your partner's needs; it's implicit attunement to each other.

And actually in some ways male couples have an advantage over straight couples: the socialization of openness and free sexuality enables the intention of trust to exist to a greater degree. The flexibility of openness forces them to deal with parts of themselves that enable going to the edge. We have a different way of expressing intimacy because some of the more primary avenues aren't part of our repertoire. For example, we may express implicit trust through leaving our mobile phone locaters on.

Gay men in couples also make different assumptions about their sex lives—both individually and together—than do straight couples. Many women, for example, feel insecure when their male partners watch porn; for gay men that's just a given, comfortable and expected.

PORNOGRAPHY

All gay men function with some assumptions and stereotypes. One prevalent theme is that for gay couples, pornography is accepted and comfortable (as opposed, for example, to heterosexual couples where it's much less acceptable). For many gay men, porn is simply a given. The questions that remain are around how it is used. Does a couple enjoy it together? Or is it a private escape? How does a couple wish to approach it?

In one sense, I believe, gay male monogamy is possible because of pornography.

To put that in context, it's important to understand that many gay couples have no role models for long-term relationships, and so they don't necessarily see sex in the context of their relationship. There are very few conversations around porn, and there are even fewer resources offering education, information, or support to male couples. Common treatment for problems within a couple is either to use drugs or alcohol to enhance their sex life, take a pill to be able to get an erection, or else to open the relationship up—as if that will make everything better.

There are still myriad questions to be answered around porn use. How do you, as a couple, want it to be part of your lives? Do you want to share it together? Enjoy it as part of your own sex rituals? Or is it private escape? How do you want to approach it? All this requires compassion, caring, and communication.

Is it something you share jointly you share with each other or is it private? Some men have special time alone for porn and self-stimulation. They announce it, build it in their schedules, make it a normal part of their lives; pornography can be a private sacred thing.

Many couples enjoy pornography jointly, especially early in the relationship. Every person has unique sexual preferences and looks for porn that reflects it, so they can explore and express that part of themselves with porn.

YOU HAVE TO BE PERFECT

Another theme is perfection. The images we have are of what we are "supposed" to look like—muscular and beautiful. And the assumption continues that, therefore, our sex lives should be modeled on porn, making them performative rather than intimate and sensory. Physical perfection in the porn industry—an accepted and treasured part of our lives—is obvious everywhere we turn.

The theme of perfection obviously finds its way into our sexual lives. Many men feel shame for having erection issues (often due to medication or normal aging) or because they cannot have orgasms. Our bodies are linked together with our expectations, and as much as we'd like to be performative, not all of us can, and none of us always can, and so anxiety or expectations of perfection lead people to feel vulnerable.

In the 1980s and 90s, gay men with AIDS started using steroids to avoid wasting. As a result, people gained muscle mass and looked ultra masculine. The technique caught on with the mainstream of gay culture expectations skyrocketed. All you have to do is look at any old media of gay men into the 80s, and you'll see a completely different aesthetic from the 70's or what we see today; we have a completely changed expectation of what masculinity should look like. And while obviously not everyone uses steroids, its usage changed the face of what we believe we should look like—and more accessibility to visual images through social media internalizing the experience of what is normal means that perception has ballooned.

And the truth is that people have by and large stopped taking public showers—so we don't even know what normal naked people look like anymore. Increased insecurity about body appearance and penis size can be correlated to the fact that we no longer socialize publicly in casual ways.

And then there's the issue of perfection being connected to age. Aging is a vulnerable topic for gay men; I am constantly hearing about people's fears of aging, as if there's a cutoff point at which desirability stops. So we plunge into the world of plastic surgery and beauty enhancements, with the underlying message: I'm not desirable enough, I'm not attractive by myself.

Most couples comprise partners who may have different levels of physical attractiveness, and almost inevitably one partner will be more secure (both in general and within the relationship) than the other. The partner with more outside affirmation of his looks will come to rely on that affirmation, while the more vulnerable one can end up feeling both insecure and resentful.

And then there's the question of open relationships...

SHOULD THE DOOR BE OPEN?

Many people think all male couples have open relationships. Talk about stereotypical assumptions! How you structure your relationship is entirely your choice as a couple. You may decide early on what you want and find as time passes that your needs both as individuals and as a couple have shifted, so the lines around openness in your relationship may become more—or less—fluid with the years.

In a sense, it's not what you do, it's how you do it. Navigating together the myriad options for structuring your relationship is more important than the actual structure itself.

Talking about open relationships is a powerful topic that provide significant territory to be explored and communicated in depth with a set of standards and agreements as part of the experience.

The agreements aren't as easy as they may seem. What does it mean to be in an open relationship? Do both partners have outside connections? Can one partner have a commitment to someone outside of the primary relationship? Can both have that commitment? How many external partners? Do the partners inform each other or not? How about sharing phone location with partners? Some men want to know details about their partners' sex lives and find them exciting, others can't bear to think about them. Are hookups one-time-only? Or can you be with a sex partner more than once? How many times? Are you comfortable with your partner going to events, meals, etc., with someone else? Or are hookups the only permitted activity?

As you can see, there are a lot of questions that demand reflection; many situations aren't clear until you're already in them.

Some couples start their relationship with the agreement; other couples agree to be monogamous to start with, leaving the option of opening up until later, so they feel it doesn't need to be discussed.

And then there are couples who think that opening their relationship is what will solve all of their problems! Not true: a crisis is the worst time to open a relationship—never do it during a difficult time.

If you're considering opening your relationship, there's a lot to think about, and I spend a lot of time in my practice talking about it.

Agreements should include parameters. Some couples accept open relationships geographically—it's okay when traveling, not at home. Still others draw other boundaries: not at our house, not in our bed. Some couples include having threesomes or orgies; others agree to not have sex unless both partners are present. In some couples, only one of the partners wishes to partake in outside sexual encounters and both partners are okay with that.

In other words, deciding is like a sliding door. You can open it as little or as much as you want. Most of my clients feel relief in hearing this because not everybody wants all of it.

Opening a relationship can highlight many of the issues we've already talked about here. What happens when one partner is more popular than the other? Open relationships can expose vulnerabilities in a relationship that can be difficult or painful for both partners. Occasionally they can make the primary relationship feel like a housemate situation. For some, the excitement of hooking up with a stranger replaces the warmth and intimacy they have at home—which is fine, as long as it's what both partners want.

A practical consideration is that sexually transmitted infections are on the rise and everyone should be tested regularly; Truvada (pRep) can now be prescribed to prevent HIV transmission. Men in relationships have ended up taking it and not telling partners, others start taking it before any activity and have told partners about it. Again, the best solution is always communicate, communicate, communicate. Also, sexually active gay men are encouraged to get tested every three months (or even more frequently if that's more comfortable) to treat STIs in case they aren't visible.

FINDING WHAT WORKS FOR YOU

Ideally, you need to prioritize the wellbeing of your own relationship and continue to have a satisfying intimate relationship together, sharing and enjoying sex. Men are good at recreational sex and have learned how to approach sex from a fun, non-emotional perspective; this can be a great strength in an open relationship. There is never a guarantee that emotional feelings for someone else won't develop over time, but we've learned how to deal with that conflict in our friendships, and can extend that awareness to our romantic partnerships.

A healthy relationship is a healthy relationship. Those that end due to a third party had other problems before the third party became an issue. I am always in favor of working on a relationship instead of splitting up.

MONOGAMY FOR GAY MEN

Yes, it exists! Some gay men don't believe it's possible, but that cynicism stems from a few factors including having been hurt by others, feeling competitive or envious with those who practice monogamy, or just plain judging others!

In earlier generations, gay men chose to live in their "gayborhoods" for socialization and emotional safety. Now, as the world is more accepting of gay male couples, it is easier to live in the suburbs and have a more mainstream life, including the white picket fence, marriage, children and monogamy. This is a privilege that earlier generations couldn't enjoy. I encourage people to choose what they want for themselves instead of listening to what others say.

Practicing monogamy doesn't mean couples aren't having or sharing sexual fantasies; they're choosing not to act on them; they often talk about who they might find hot, and use fantasy or pornography together. And some may open up over time, just as some open relationships can later become monogamous.

ACCEPTING AND COMMUNICATING PREFERENCES

Given the struggles men have at first recognizing their own needs, and then speaking, there's a whole lot of avoidance going on. By the time they come to me in therapy, there are walls that have gone up; some have fought and others have drifted apart from each other.

No one has taught either of you to be vulnerable. Small surprise that you don't know how to do it!

To one extent or another, we all have difficulties owning our desires and speaking to each other about sexuality and sexual issues. Doing so requires honesty, self-disclosure, and understanding the potential of hurting your partner or of breaking up.

DEVELOPING INTIMACY RITUALS, ENJOYING SEX FOR SEX

Intimacy rituals aren't necessarily for having sex at all. They are for maintaining a connection. Designating some special time together on an ongoing basis is one of the best ways of keeping your sex life interesting and intimate.

Some couples have specified date nights where they carve out time to do something special together—go out for dinner, to the movies, to the theatre, or just stay in and have a romantic candlelight dinner—which take precedence in their schedules.

Others do weekly check-ins to talk about how things are going, what's been going on in terms of their sexual lives, what things have become problematic or are especially good, what they may be learning together.

Whatever you choose to do together, make sure that it's intentional and regular, so you don't lose touch with your attraction to each other. Here are some tips for how you might structure your intimacy ritual:

The task of being in a couple is the ability to recognize what you want, what you need, and to recognize and even celebrate all forms of intimacy—"touch time" together, downtime, and sexuality. The goal is to strengthen what exists interpersonally between the two of you.

The challenge, of course, is in being able to speak about preferences while finding a way to show respect, appreciation, and assertiveness all at once.

DISCUSSION POINTS AND QUESTIONS TO SHARE

Each of you can take a turn sharing your responses to the discussion points below and appreciate how honesty and vulnerability will help you grow together. You may also choose to write out your answers—whatever works best for you.

Individual and couple questions

What do I enjoy with our intimate and sexual routine?

_____

_____

_____

_____

_____

_____

Am I upfront about my preferences so my partner knows I like the thing I like?

_____

_____

_____

_____

_____

_____

How often do I assume my partner can read my mind when we're being sexual?

_____

_____

_____

_____

_____

_____

_____

What are the things that are hard to talk about that I could be more upfront about?

_____

_____

_____

_____

_____

_____

_____

Couple:

What do we both know we like about our sex life?

_____

_____

_____

_____

_____

_____

_____

_____

How can we work on establishing a meaningful connection as part of our sexual experience? To expand our intimacy

_____

_____

_____

_____

_____

_____

_____

_____

Are we okay with the rituals we have or do we want to expand them?

_____

_____

_____

_____

_____

_____

_____

Can we both commit to taking greater emotional and verbal risks with each other about what's working and what we want?

_____

_____

_____

_____

_____

_____

_____

TODAY'S TIPS

Remember that a healthy intimate relationship that decides to open up requires mutual security and trust. You need to honestly assess whether the two of you are in a space to take this risk. Generally, solid secure couples can handle the risk of opening up their relationships if they choose to do so. Also, partners in a solid relationship don't necessarily fall in love with others and want to leave when their intimate partnership is strong. The relationship remains the priority.

Another point to keep in mind is that each of you in changing the boundaries of the relationship have a duty to yourselves and each other to really listen to yourself when considering a hookup. For example, if you are getting a vibe from a hook up that something doesn't feel right, or you are uncomfortable for any reason, listen to this and look elsewhere. People sometimes forget that there are other men out there and healthier people to choose from.

🔑🔑 TODAY'S TIPS

Below are some tips for navigating an open relationship if you are considering it:

- **Your relationship comes first.** Agree to make your intimate and sexual relationship the priority. It is easy to get caught up in the excitement of new possibilities and diminish intimacy and emotional needs of y our partnership. Remind yourselves that your healthy relationship is the priority.

- **Communication is essential.** Talk to each other to negotiate your terms and to ascertain if your relationship is solid enough to be opened up. Periodically revisit how this is working and be honest with yourselves about this.

- **Remember the truths about long term intimacy.** The difference between a new hookup and the predictability of a long-term relationship is vast. Be realistic in your expectations and comparisons. Many people in relationships fear there is no spark left in comparison to connecting with a stranger, this isn't necessarily accurate.

- **Decide how much to share.** There isn't a rule here for all relationships. It is up to you both to evaluate what you want. Some couples enjoy sharing the details of their hookups outside and use that to enhance the erotic aspect of their relationship. Other couples don't want to know that details for a variety of reasons and prefer to have a "Don't Ask Don't Tell" policy. And some couples take an approach that is between these two.

- **Your bed is sacred.** Even if you have sex with others in your bed, you want to maintain a bond and connection between you and your partner that is special and strong. Maintain your intimate space as a couple and decide with clarity about where it is okay to be sexual with others; such as away from home, out of town, or going out alone. Respecting these agreements will make this challenge easier.

- **How many times are allowed?** This too varies from couple to couple. It depends on each of your levels of security and comfort. Some couples have a rule that hooks up are okay but not more than once with someone, or no dates. Other couples are comfortable with repeat performances but limit that to a number of times, whereas others have no limits on how often.

- **Strangers or friends?** Is it acceptable to hook up with friends who either partner may know, or strangers only? Set a boundary according to your preferences and stick to with this in deference to each other. Like other tips, there is no right or wrong way here, it depends on your personal and joint preferences.

- **Prioritize safety.** Adhere to safer sex guidelines outside of your relationship such as and getting tested for STI's and HIV on a regular basis (every three months is considered the norm but more often based upon your sexual activities is also wise. It is also suggested that sexually open partners who have anal sex outside should take Prep (Truvada) in-order to greatly reduce the risks of HIV infection. If you slip, get tested out of respect to your partner and yourself.

- **Trial period.** I always remind people that nothing is written in stone. Try this out for an agreed upon period of time and see how it goes. Many couples often decide to discontinue this. If you need help, don't forget to consult with your friends or a therapist

- **The bumpy road. Having an open relationship is difficult.** Partners who can tolerate some confusion or jealousy are more apt to handle this, but it is still challenging. Be reassured that it isn't just smooth sailing and there are many variables to manage with each other, including health communication for how it is working.

Your Sexuality, Reflection and Communication

This guided meditation focuses on leading you through a process of self-discovery and comfort in relation to your sexuality. It encourages honest self-assessment as well as assessment and attunement with each other.

If you'd like to listen to Rick guiding you through this meditation, either alone or together, scan the code here:

Just take a moment and get comfortable in your seat, allowing your body to inform you exactly what is the right position for you to be present and comfortable.

Excellent.

Just take a few deep breaths, settling in and settling down, appreciating that with each out breath you can breathe away any tightness and tension, and with each in breath you can take in calm.

And as you venture into the topic of sexuality, you may feel a tightness inside or fear, this is not an unusual response to dealing with sex.

But first, allow yourself to find your way into comfort. Excellent.

No need to worry. Instead, just allow yourself to settle into comfort and train your body to be able to be neutral when it comes to exploring sexuality and eroticism, that's right,

Instead of being on alert, instead of shutting down, you get to find your way into comfort. And the way that you find your comfort is by taking a few moments of settling in first.

This is the way to begin. This is the way to continue. This is the way to be successful. Allow your belly to be soft, allow each breath to be nice and deep, and rhythmic, settling in, letting go of tightness in your neck and shoulders and exhaling extra deeply.

Appreciate comfort, and as you find your way, you recognize that the best way to work on challenges is from the space of comfort, good job.

And as you think about your own sexuality, notice the ways in which your body tells you something. Do you feel tightness or tension as a result? Or do you feel excitement?

Just be attentive to whatever it is you notice because there's no right or wrong answer.

Your truth is that you get to navigate your own world. You get to navigate your sexual life within your body. From the inside the space of yourself.

And as you sit and breathe and recognize that being inside of yourself isn't an unusual space for you. Your body is home. A place where you breathe, live, eat, a place where you sleep.

And when you feel sexual urges, befriend yourself. Allow yourself to appreciate that this place that you inhabit is a place that you know very, very well. This place is feels good for you. And just as you get to enjoy each breath, you get to appreciate when you're hungry, when you feel satisfied, and what you enjoy. Allow yourself to do the same with sexuality. That's right.

What is it that you enjoy? What is it that you don't enjoy? What is it that you tolerate in the spirit of others but may not be your own preferences? Be honest with yourself. Even if you've never admitted to others, or your partner what you want.

This is your own time of exploration. Your body is your home. You get to appreciate what it is that you like most. Notice what you're coming up with. What parts of your likes to be touched. What parts of your body do you like to be touched, and is it a soft touch or an intense touch? What makes you feel good?

The key to being sexual and enjoying sex is to know exactly what works for you, and part of the challenge around healthy sexuality is also being good to yourself. Being good to yourself means enjoying sensations, recognizing discomfort and asserting yourself with others. Being good to yourself means being able to represent yourself when you like what you're doing. That's right.

You get to say yes when yes is what you want, and you get to say no when no is what you need. Instead of being caught up in being subservient or pleasing, you get to enjoy what you want. You deserve this to get what you want and to ask for it. That's right.

If you can think about one or two things in this moment that you would enjoy, allow them to trickle up into your awareness. Imagine that you are able to find a way to speak about these things with your partner. What may seem daunting in this moment perhaps is doable. Being relaxed and centered within your body allows you to know things and ask for things that you might not normally ask for. Go for it. Be true to yourself, be honest, be clear. Feel the inspiration inside.

Find the words to describe to your partner what you're thinking about or what you're fantasizing about, or what simply would feel good for you. Excellent.

Notice how it feels to enable yourself to have the space to do this. Is it something that you feel good about? Or is it something that scares you? We've all been conditioned in our histories to minimize our sexual feelings as a result of growing up in a world where we knew we were different. And instead of minimizing this, you get to enjoy it now, to amplify it now because it's what you want.

Appreciate that part of being a have a healthy sexual being is feeling absolutely fine about your preferences, your needs and your desires. That's right. There is no feeling, there is no fantasy that you shouldn't have. You get to be you. You be you. That's right. Appreciate that more is possible for you now.

What you might have been hiding from yourself or hiding from your partner can be in the realm of possibilities, and it can go well. Excellent.

And now focus on your partner for a bit. He may not be near you, but you can feel his presence, and you can feel the awareness of his body next to you. And as you're honest with yourself, you can appreciate what it is that he wants for himself even if it isn't spoken about. Is it that he wants a certain position or a certain way of being touched, or that he wants you to connect with him in a certain way, or that he is threatened by a connection with you and keeps his distance, instead of simply being reactive or defensive, allow yourself to see him in this moment with a greater sense of clarity, and in this moment, it isn't up to you to fix or make do, just allow yourself to see him and understand him from a different vantage point. For right now, that's all. Excellent.

It may seem difficult at other moments to allow yourself to see him in the way that you do now, but now you get him. And there may be a part of you that wants to give him what he needs and wants to please him. This is coming from your own generosity, Allow yourself to imagine that pleasing him actually brings you joy. Instead of fighting or competing you get to enjoy the sensations of giving him something that makes him feel good, that enables him to feel good. Yes, sometimes it's just this simple. Excellent.

Appreciate that you can be a little more attuned to him, and imagine that he can ask for what he needs with a greater sense of ease, because he can feel your presence in a different way and take the risk of asking for what he wants, and you can be okay with this in this very moment. That's right.

Check in with your body now. What are the ways in which you're feeling relaxed and open? How does it feel different from the way that you feel at other times? Appreciate any subtle shift that's taken place inside of you as a result of doing this work. Excellent.

Remember that you have an ability to go into a deeper place inside in order to navigate the world of sexuality and eroticism with your partner, and there's always room for minute changes and improvements, and frequently, just doing a little bit more can make all the difference for the two of you to feel more appreciative and more connected. Making some changes now may not feel like that big of a deal but will yield you even more in the long run- more connection, love, respect, more tolerance, just more.

Picture the two of you becoming a little bit closer to each other, connected and appreciative in a way that is what each of you have wanted. Maybe you've protected yourselves from each other. Instead of keeping distance and maintaining the protection, enter into each other's awareness with pleasure. Enter into your own zone of awareness, where you can enjoy the fact that each of you can be there for each other in a way that's just a little bit closer, just a little more tender, or even just a little more hot, or all of the above, if that's what you'd like.

Check in with your body once again. Appreciate the ways in which comfort is reassuring to you. Even though a part of you may feel like you need to shut down, another part of you can show up, be present and enjoy the energy that is yours now. And together you will enjoy this gain. That's right.

Your body is your home. His body is his home. Together you create a beautiful home—together. Excellent.

Before coming back, just take a few deep easy breaths, appreciating the journey you've just had. Acknowledge to yourself that the growth that you've experienced will enable you to approach things just a little bit differently. You have the strength to do so, and the success of doing this will pay off. Success only brings more success. Excellent.

Also, before coming back to the outside world, take a few breaths, wiggle your fingers and toes just to land in your body once again, imagining what it will be look imagining what it will look like once you open your eyes. And when the moment feels right and you feel ready, just bring yourself back to the outside world, coming back, gently coming back, slowly, opening your eyes, returning to awake, alert and fully present. Welcome back!

CHAPTER 6

Money and Finances

It's a truism that most arguments and conflicts within a relationship—gay or straight—usually start with money. And sadly, when relationships end and divorce looms, all the couple's issues come out in one place—money. All that makes your financial life together an essential topic.

The most important factor here is communications and agreements, starting as early in the relationship as you can manage. Having conversations about money, expenses, preferences and savings can keep things running smoothly in your household and alleviate a lot of conflict and pain.

CHALLENGES OF TWO MEN MELDING LIVES

So by now you probably have a pretty good idea not just about the characteristics of male couples in general, but also about some of the issues and behaviors special to the couple in which you find yourself.

Money and finances present some unique challenges for men, and can contribute significant stress to your relationship.

Again, you are two men. How you were raised, as males, and the expectations that were part of your upbringing included what your roles and responsibilities would be in life on a financial level. Even if it was never articulated in your family, there were assumptions baked into your childhood and adolescence.

In fact, money is particularly interesting because it's an area where those assumptions are never questioned, even for those of us fortunate enough to have been raised by parents accepting of our being gay! Males were—and perhaps still are—expected to be financially successful and to be the principal provider in their marriage, relationship, and/or family.

The imagine of a strong man always entails financial independence and even dominance.

Even in the 21st century, there's still a heteronormative expectation about the role of a man and money. It may be a relic of the past where the husband was the breadwinner and supported the family, and the wife managed the household finances and those associated with children, but for many people that is still the reality and for all of us it's a framework that casts a long shadow.

Male couples have absolutely no training around—or models of—how to manage money between them. Some unconsciously fall into old roles they learned from books, movies, television, or their experience of their families of origin. Others find it a constant source of worry, jealousy, and struggle. No one is unaffected.

And public male couplehood is a relatively new phenomenon, at least in the United States. Before same-sex marriage became legal, there wasn't much incentive to merge finances, and a whole lot of reasons to not do it. Even mentioning a male partner as the beneficiary of an insurance policy or estate could be awkward; many men didn't want their company's HR department to know they lived with another man.

Additionally, the pressures of keeping up with the gay male stereotype is challenging for many, especially if you don't have oodles of money. You may want to like as though you fit in just like the proverbial them, but may have struggles actually doing so financially.

SEPARATE OR TOGETHER?

Because of this lack of a model, when a male couple decides to live together or get married, they can find themselves floundering. It's a truism that finances are the least-discussed area of common life for everyone, gay or straight; but that reticence and avoidance are compounded for gay men because, as we've seen, we're not the best communicators within our relationships as it is; adding a hot button like money into the mix isn't going to make talking any easier.

In fact, partly because of the competitiveness ingrained in us as men, male partners are often more private and about their money than heterosexuals. They may not have much financial literacy; they may have an uncomfortable income gap; they may not be comfortable having any kind of financial dependency on another person. The easiest and least confrontational response is to just not talk about it: each partner keeps his own accounts and does his own thing to pay bills.

Of course it is cleaner and easier to have a merged account, at the very least for running the household—but even this reasonably innocuous step often doesn't happen. In the decades before marriage equality became the law of certain states and eventually of the country, two men sharing a checking account was often embarrassing and even contentious.

These days, when many couples feel fine about the public-facing nature of their relationship, there's a hidden side-effect of legalization: no one wants to model themselves on heterosexual couples and the notion of merger feels for some like totally "falling in."

There are of course options, and choices that can be made. You may choose to keep all your money matters separate, and behave financially like housemates. You may choose to throw everything in together—savings, checking, money markets, home ownership—and assume you'll never want to divide it up again. The middle way is to keep some accounts your own, and set up a separate joint household account out of which you pay for common goods and services. And there's a whole spectrum of possibilities even within each of those categories.

ANSWERING THE HARD QUESTIONS

Life is never as simple as figuring out how to pay the bills. There are a lot of considerations behind simply "paying the bills" that go far deeper into your identity as individuals and as a couple.

For example, most men don't come to the relationship as financial equals. You've made career choices that have brought you in different directions, and the end result might be a marked inequality of income. How do you deal with that? Splitting everything fifty-fifty may or may not make sense in the face of income inequality.

The easiest thing to do for many is at least have a household account that is used for day-to-day expenses, where each partner contributes a decided-on amount. But this is very basic and doesn't cover everything.

Other finances are equally difficult to navigate. For those who have the means to save money, or have a 401K through work, how is it decided what should be done with this money once retirement actually takes place? Should it be shared jointly? Or is it considered the property of the individual?

There are no right answers. What works for one couple might not for another. The key to making your decisions work for you is in your communication. Talk about the how and the why; share your past ideas about money; talk about your dreams for the future. And even once you've made your financial decisions, check back with them and with each other frequently. Needs change over time, and there's no choice that cannot be revisited.

LOSS OF POWER IS THE METAPHOR

Again, many man are not great communicators, and some couples would rather avoid the whole topic in general instead of deciding on a plan that works well for both partners and maintains an easy way to manage expenses.

For many people, keeping money separate is preferable as a way to maintain power or control. It may serve as a metaphor for having power, or actually feel like it. Considering merging money can feel like a total loss of control.

One common dynamic I see with my clientele involves a partner who makes more than the other by significant amounts. This can contribute to power dynamics, where the more successful one feels as though he has more power to make certain decisions that really ought to be joint decisions, or for the partner who is less successful financially to feel powerless and or resentful. He may not feel as though he has the right to speak strongly about things that are important to him, or acquiesce with some resentment to his partner. In a healthy partnership, significant decisions are made jointly. Some couples with disparate incomes feel that is okay to give the wealthier partner more deciding power. I always encourage clear communication and taking both needs into account under these circumstances.

Think about keeping things separate for this moment.

- **Is that what you do in your couple?**
- **Does it feel preferable?**
- **Or does it not make any sense?**
- **Are these things you normally discuss?**
- **Who actually pays the bills?**

- **What does it mean to not discuss some of these basic topics with each other?**

- **Who and what are you protecting?**

I recently worked with a couple going through the process of divorce and in deciding to work with a mediator or lawyers, it was made clear that legally all expenses and savings would be considered in deciding how much each partner gets, whereas with the mediator decisions were not made on legal rights, but on agreements that partners breaking up agree upon. With this couple, the higher wage earner who saved more money felt strongly that he should keep his own individual investments since he earned it himself. This would not hold up well in a court of law, but worked well for these partners who were ending the relationship.

AVOIDANCE OF TALKING ABOUT FINANCES

I worked with a couple who had been together close to 20 years, and in all those years had kept things separate—and I mean completely separate. Both had their own jobs, hadn't revealed all these years who much they earned, nor did they discuss how much money they had individually saved over the years, and it was agreed upon in my office that each of their money was okay to be kept separate. I worked with them to increase their communication on many fronts, especially regarding money. My hope was that their overly independent lifestyles might merge more for the wellbeing of the couple.

CULTURAL OR FAMILY DIFFERENCES

Given that culture and families have their own modes of how they deal with money, it's natural that the two of you may come to your relationship with very different assumptions about how to handle money. Many if not most of us come from backgrounds—either cultural or familial—in which finances were never discussed. We didn't have the opportunity to learn because no one was teaching us, giving us a model for how to handle family finances. Some cultures and families seek to keep their financial situation hidden; others flaunt it. This can get very confusing as you think about the choices you want to make, both for yourself as an individual, but also for the two of you as a couple.

So the first thing you need to do is acknowledge and explore that history. What assumptions do you each make? How were those assumptions informed? It is especially important for couples to have detailed conversations about how they were taught to behave regarding money based on their families and cultures of origin. Given that it is one of the more powerful modes for disagreements between partners, it is especially important to understand how your partner was raised regarding financial views and how money stress was dealt with. The idea is to appreciate differences, and to experience empathy towards your partner's experiences since this is such a powerful and vulnerable topic.

Some cultures value financial success and the appearance of it, while others value quietness and privacy or even secrecy around finances. These are two extremes that you might not even have thought to question.

I am frequently surprised that when I take my clients' words regarding their anxieties about money at face value, sometimes I realize they are minimizing the danger they are in for getting by, whereas for others, their anxiety may be a way they learned to be in the world regarding money even though they may not need to worry as much as they are. So the two extremes show up every day in people's lives.

Recognize how you were raised and by whom, and what you learned from them. Explore together your ideas about money, and see how your views can affect your partner.

BUT GAY MEN ARE RICH, RIGHT?

It's a myth that all male couples are financially stable or even wealthy. Sometimes from the outside it looks as though all gay couples are successful, but that can be a façade they put up. Given the significance of outward appearance in the gay culture, and the number of successful men who have means to live well and show it, frequently couples who have financial issues peg themselves in a different category than other gay couples and may diminish themselves or feel as though they don't fit into the gay community. This only reinforces inferiority issues that already are prevalent for gay men in general. A healthier—but more difficult—approach is to learn to value successes in a number of ways that go beyond financial means.

MAKING PURCHASES

Spending is tricky for everyone. Anyone who's ever had to stick to a budget can tell you that!

Purchases affect both of you. It's pretty easy to decide together that you need to replace a broken appliance; it's less straightforward when you want different material things, luxuries, or nonessentials. I have seen couples lose confidence in each other and even their marriages over a partner's spending habits. The other end of the spectrum is the need to control your partner's spending, peering at bank statements and demanding to know what every ten dollars went to.

A healthy relationship, to my mind, is one in which the big expenses are agreed upon and budgeted, but where neither partner is obligated to check in with the other for every small expenditure. We aren't here to dictate how our partners spend their disposable income, but rather to be clear about what is and isn't actually "disposable."

WHAT HAPPENS WHEN THERE'S A PROBLEM?

There may be a myriad of reasons why having an issue with spending can be common for male couples. Appreciating that for many of us, our upbringing has included pain and trauma, and buying things and having a nice wardrobe, car, home or furnishings inside simply feels good!

People have a spending issue or compulsion for many reasons and engage in behaviors in a variety of ways including collections of many sorts, pornography, real estate, and things that validate external worthiness. There may be a whole lot being compensated for based on internal histories.

More likely is that one member of the couple has a spending issue and has gone to great lengths to keep it secretive, but somehow gets caught, time and time again. The goal is to take responsibility as an individual and create a way to work on this and progress, without having to justify or prove self to partner.

Additionally, the pressures of keeping up with the gay male stereotype is challenging for many, especially if you don't have oodles of money. You may want to like as though you fit in just like the proverbial "them," but may have struggles actually doing so financially.

DO WHAT WORKS FOR YOU

There is no rule about how to effectively manage money as a gay couple. The specifics are up to you based on your own sensibilities. What is most important, is that things actually get discussed rather than buried, and that you create some type of structure that involves keeping track and checking in regarding spending and finances for both of you. Keeping these conversations ongoing will add to a myriad of healthy aspects in your relationship also keep your money issues current between you both.

Your ideal outcome may not be to merge, or to keep separate, but rather to discuss the realities of your finances.

There is no rule about how to effectively manage money as a gay couple. The specifics are up to you, based on your own sensibilities. What is most important is that things actually get discussed rather than buried, and that you create some type of structure that involves keeping track and checking in regarding spending and finances for both of you. Keeping these conversations ongoing will add to a myriad of healthy aspects in your relationship also keep your money issues current between you.

DISCUSSION POINTS AND QUESTIONS TO SHARE

Each of you can take a turn sharing your responses to the discussion points below and appreciate how honesty and vulnerability will help you grow together. You may also choose to write out your answers—whatever works best for you.

Can we agree to the following: instead of burying our money tensions we will bring them to the surface and deal with them?

_____

_____

_____

_____

_____

_____

Can we each identify our vulnerabilities and bad habits regarding money and will speak about them openly with each other?

_____

_____

_____

_____

_____

_____

As it's such a powerful topic, can we agree to approach it with respect and minimize accusations against each other?

_____

_____

_____

_____

We get to carve out our own way of dealing rather than the model we learned from our families

_____

_____

_____

_____

_____

We get to do the same in relation to the gay community—we get to do it our way.

_____

_____

_____

_____

_____

TODAY'S TIPS

- When it comes to money there's no right way, it's your own way, and you both need to decide how much blending will take place and how you might have your own accounts for your own spending.

- Each of you can start by identifying your spending and savings styles, and how you'd like to continue improving them.

- Once you've identified your style, designate more time to discuss your individual styles with each other even before you find a solution

- Designate a more concrete plan as a couple to merge a portion of your assets that takes care of day-to-day expenses, entertainment, and travel.

- Decide whether as a couple you also want to designate a concrete plan to save money jointly

Shifting How You Deal with Finances

This guided meditation focuses on leading you through a process of self-discovery and comfort in relation to your attitudes towards money. It encourages honest self-assessment.

If you'd like to listen to Rick guiding you through this meditation, either alone or together, scan the code here:

Choose a nice comfortable seat for yourself and take a few deep breaths. As you do this, notice the tension inside your body. You know what this topic is about, and money is simply a subject that evokes discomfort and avoidance.

In this moment, instead of feeling discomfort, allow yourself to expand into comfort. By breathing deeply, by softening your belly, by continuing to breathe in...and out...in an exaggerated way.

That's right.

As you take this time to settle in, you recognize that your body becomes more and more comfortable, little by little. Good.

It really isn't that hard to settle in. You've gotten more accustomed to doing this with each chapter, and within a few short moments, you notice is that the space of calm and wellbeing envelopes you. And before you know it, you have switched from tense to comfortable.

Good job.

And as you take this time for yourself, appreciate that just thinking about money is a topic that causes to want to escape. But instead of escaping, you remain present, still and quiet, and you are very comfortable now which is a really nice experience. You are taking full advantage of this positive opportunity.

As you expand these sensations of comfort, you can begin to appreciate that you allow yourself to embrace the topic of money, which normally results in avoidance or shut down . Instead, you are open to exploration. That is right. You are willing to see the truth and face what needs to be faced. Good for you.

There is nobody out there who doesn't have the challenge of managing money, or taking care of details and everybody has moments of shame about the ways that they deal with money. You are hardly alone.

Because you are in a partnership, it is especially important that each of you settles into facing your personal finances with a great deal of understanding and organization, and that you both take the same

approach in however you decide to approach this together.
That is right.

Each of you in your partnership gets to decide what works best for
you both. For some that means keeping things separate, and coming
up with a certain amount to meet monthly expenses, and for other
couple it means reporting in with each other about all expenses, while
negotiating how it is going and where money will be spent.

For many other people, in between is where you may land. You get
to decide what is best for you, and how you would like to proceed.
Excellent.

Notice what you are feeling in this moment. How did your body shift
or your breathing change? Were you aware of tension creeping back in
as you began to think about this?

Just continue to breathe, maintaining this steady feeling of relaxation.
Good job.

Since there isn't a right way or a wrong way, take this time to be open
to yourself about an arrangement that works best. How can you make
things run more smoothly for the two for you as a couple? Does it
involve having more conversations, or deducting more money from
your accounts, or saving more money for each billing cycle, or ways to
make more money.

Whatever it means for you, be honest. And as you are taking
inventory in this moment, appreciate that how you first learned to

*deal with money stemmed from your family of origin. Appreciate this.
Was money scarce or plentiful? Was it talked about or avoided? Were
decisions made privately or jointly?*

*No doubt, there was some bit of stress regarding money in your
family, and now you have the opportunity to change things just a bit,
and create your own way of dealing with financial issues between
both of you.*

*Think about a time where the two of you negotiated something
difficult, perhaps not even about money. And how good it felt to get
through it, to get beyond the tension, and to reach a resolve where you
both returned to normal again. Notice the incident that you came up
with. It is easy to remember and appreciate this time, and enjoy the
good feelings from resolving some tension that felt difficult. You both
had the skills to negotiate and grow back then, and you can certainly
do that again. That is right. Notice how it feels inside your body
remember this. You don't have to reinvent the wheel, instead just go
back to an earlier success and bring it forward to the now.*

*You can do the same with finances. You can find a way to challenge
yourself and have these really difficult conversations- to really listen to
each other and come up with solutions that are better than you have
decided upon at this point.*

*Every couple has room for improvement. There is no need to feel
shame about this, just recognize that you are not alone and that
making some improvements will help. It is that simple. Excellent.*

Appreciate where you are in this very moment, and how different it feels compared to the moment when you first began this exercise. You have expanded your mind and your body into the zone of possibility, and as a result of this possibility, you can imagine new thoughts, new conversations and new rituals. The order of your life can shift into organization and communication.

Take a few more moments and think what you will do to make some shifts and changes regarding your finances or your spending. This is simply a start for you to take note of, and go from there. Appreciate the clarity, the honesty, and the relief from knowing that instead of shutting down, you can do more and you get to do more. Appreciate the relief that this brings to you in this very moment, as well as in your future. Good.

And now embrace one of the many moments when you and your partner are sitting down and you have made it your priority to hear each other differently. You can choose to get along better with each other, to respect each other's ideas, and to come up with one or two or new approaches for your spending and your finances. The relief that this brings implies success and the level of intimacy that you share increases as a result.

This is doable, this can be one of your many successes. Great work!

Now simply begin the process of reorienting yourself by taking a few final breaths, wiggling your toes and fingers, imaging what your room will look like once you open your eyes, and when are you ready, open your eyes slowly, bringing yourself back to the outside world. Great.

Conclusion

Congratulations on getting through this workbook! I hope that you'll keep referring back to using tips and exercises to keep your relationship solid and strong.

This resource can serve as a toolkit and guide as you allow yourself to explore your challenges rather than avoiding them. All you need in addition is a little intention to work on your relationship together, I think you'll find that growth comes easily and your mutual experiences of your relationship will grow as well.

As you can probably tell now that you've moved through this workbook, I believe the key to a successful and happy relationship is communication. Silence and avoidance are not your friends and do not help your well being. In the short term it may feel easier to avoid, but in the long term it erodes at the success of your relationship.

No need to make communication feel formal and separate from the rest of your lives. You undoubtedly spend time in the car together; seize that time to check in with each other. Meals, evening routines, Saturday mornings—there's no set schedule you need to follow; you just need to keep communication flowing.

We all know the advice that abounds for heterosexual couples doesn't always fit gay relationships. That's why I wrote this workbook; it's why I speak at conferences and present workshops, often to professionals in the mental-health field, to share the specific needs, challenges, and joys of LGBTQ+ relationships. And it's why I have a thriving virtual private practice and see couples literally all over the world to help them manage the specific strengths and challenges they are facing.

All of this is to say: you are not alone. You are seen. Your relationship deserves to thrive. I hope this workbook will help you embrace who you are as individuals and as a couple, and will become a resource for you for years to come.

If you have enjoyed some of these exercises and noticed that your partnership has thrived with greater communication, consider doing individual therapy if you would like to explore more deeply how your history has impacted your behaviors in your relationship. Or, in order to continue on your quest to be a healthier couple, consider any modality of couples work such as couples therapy, a couples group, or a couples retreat.

Success in your couple will be an ongoing process—and you deserve to have the best relationship possible!!

DISCUSSION POINTS AND QUESTIONS TO SHARE

Each of you can take a turn sharing your responses to the discussion points below and appreciate how honesty and vulnerability will help you grow together. You may also choose to write out your answers—whatever works best for you.

How have you changed as an individual from reading this book and using some of the exercises?

_____

_____

_____

_____

_____

_____

How have you as a couple become stronger as a result of reading and using the suggestions offered in this workbook?

_____

_____

_____

_____

_____

_____

What will you continue to work on (alone or together) to maintain growth that you have accomplished?

_____

_____

_____

_____

_____

_____

_____

Which topics need more work from these chapters, and specifically how will you continue to chip away at these areas needing individual and joint growth?

_____

_____

_____

_____

_____

_____

_____

How has your communication become easier as a result of insights and suggestions from this workbook?

_____

_____

_____

_____

_____

_____

_____

_____

_____

_____

_____

_____

_____

_____

_____

_____

# TODAY'S TIPS

- The saying "relationships are a lot of work" is no joke! (What does this really mean anyways?). Keep the promise to continue to make efforts to remain connected to each other and to keep communication fresh so you both can enjoy what you have together.

- Being in love shifts and changes over the years. Moving from fireworks to a more mellow connection and commitment is normal and healthy.

- Always prioritize your partnership. Be respectful and careful in how you represent your partner and your couplehood. Sacred is important and healthy!

- Addressing tensions early on adds to the wellbeing of your partnership. Letting then go for too long erodes happiness.

- Enjoy moments together that feel good! This is the glue that makes your relationship strong!

Guided Meditation
New Directions

We've been on quite a journey in this workbook! In this final meditation, you'll take the time to appreciate what you've experienced about communicating with each other, giving each other a safe space, and finding new ways to solve old problems.

If you'd like to listen to Rick guiding you through this meditation, either alone or together, scan the code here:

Take a few moments for yourself and get comfortable. Settle in perfectly, your body knows just the right position for you in this moment. Closing your eyes, gently and slowly, that's right.

Now exhale a smooth relaxed breath and notice how good it feels to begin to let go. Allowing each exhale and each inhale to become a little deeper, and noticing how your body is settling into this peace and quiet in a way that feels wonderful.

How quickly you are able to do this now! After just a few moments of clock time, you have taught yourself how to bring yourself to a state of bliss in just a matter of moments. Good for you.

Just focus and appreciate the feeling of satisfaction right here and right now. You did it! You learned how good it feels to use your body to help you feel good, and to use this state of mindfulness to explore ways to be even more resourceful in your life and in your relationship. It works! Good for you.

Appreciate your journey. What has it meant for you to use the chapters from this workbook as your guide?

Experience the shift of where you were when you started working from this book, and where you are now. Good.

Progress is slow and steady, yet noticing it and acknowledging it only brings even more success. Success only brings more success. Enjoy this awareness inside and all over.

Enjoy this moment to appreciate where you have come to. Even with more to do, you are able to enjoy what you have accomplished- which conversations you and your partner had that were helpful, which guided meditations enabled you to explore something more deeply, and how or why this has been helpful for you. Excellent.

Allow your body to feel the shifts and changes you have made. Also appreciate that not only is it you that has made changes, so have both of you as a couple. Appreciate the ways in which both of you have come together just a little bit more. That is right. Joining in vision and commitment, feeling more connected and intent on doing well with each other. Take this in and enjoy it, you are making this happen and will only continue to flourish and grow.

Notice that as you take stock of this progress, even though there is more to do, and you will continue doing this on your own, it feels good to move along from where you were to where you are now. In this moment you get to enjoy the feelings of satisfaction and you don't even need to worry about more growth, it will simply happen.

You know that there have been other times in your life where you set out to do things, and over time you were able to reach your goals, and then did even more. It will happen with the two of you, just like these earlier times.

Good job. Being more open and communicate has paid off and will continue too. Enjoy the good feeling inside, right here and right now. Excellent.

Appreciate the feeling of satisfaction and progress, and know that when you open your eyes in a moment, the progression will simply continue effortlessly and easily effortlessly and easily.

When you are ready, prepare to bring yourself back, gently and slowly. Wiggling your fingers and toes, beginning to orient yourself to the outside world, coming back, opening your eyes, returning back.

Excellent. Welcome back!

NEXT STEPS: What Rick Recommends

You've already experienced many benefits and gains from doing this workbook together. But this isn't the end! This is the beginning of what you will continue to do, and can do on your own.

If you're thinking about therapy, there are a few things to consider:

- **Individual vs couples?**
- **Should the therapist be gay or straight?**
- **How to find gay therapists**

There are tremendous benefits to either short-term or ongoing therapy, and I encourage you to explore them. Remember that doing this work makes your life and relationship more harmonious.

Enjoy!

ABOUT THE AUTHOR

Rick Miller, LICSW, has dedicated his 40-year career to motivating people to change and inspiring them to find optimism inside themselves. Through his work as a psychotherapist, public speaker, podcaster, workshop presenter, interviewer, and author, he helps individuals, couples, groups, and others connect—and thrive—together.

A gay man who has himself navigated social stigma, Rick's journey of self-acceptance has influenced his work with others. He shows people how to embrace complexities as well as vulnerabilities—and how to grow from these experiences. Rick is a sought-after speaker for events, workshops, and conferences. He is the founder and executive director of a nonprofit organization, Gay Sons & Mothers, and the executive producer of the documentary, *Mom, I Have Something to Tell You.*

An acclaimed collaborator and subject-matter leader, Rick shares his expertise through numerous mediums.

- **as a columnist for Psychology Today and a frequent contributor to Psychotherapy Networker, Medium, and Psychotherapy.net**

- **as a TEDx speaker**

- **by partnering with well-known couples experts Terry Real, Esther Perel, and Stan Tatkin**

- **through participation in the prestigious Harvard Couples Conference and The Couples Conference**

He's available to speak at your next conference, workshop, or retreat.

ACKNOWLEDGEMENTS

I have been inspired by many wonderful mentors, helpers, and friends in my career as a couples' therapist.

Thank you to my parents, Samuel and Suzanne Miller, who portrayed true coupledom: happiness, warmth, tolerance, prioritizing, conflict resolution, and humor.

Early on in my career I learned that being an interactive therapist and having more than one person in the room was stimulating and fruitful. Along the way I had mentors and great friends who helped me grow: Terry Real, Jeffrey Zeig, Esther Perel, Michele Weiner-Davis, Stan Takin, and Lilian Borges.

I am grateful for all past and current couples who trusted—and continue to trust—me enough to speak their truths and teach me the realities about couple-hood with male couples. I continue to learn and grow from working with you.

Thank you to my master class family for constantly encouraging me to continue to grow and flourish. And thanks to Martha Stark who always encourages me to share my couple' theories in writing and teaching.

I have shared cases with colleagues whose professional approach has been encouraging: Tanya Cherkerzian, Michael Burke, Karen Greenberg, Chris Shea, Ramona Dvorak, Justin Hecht, Rory Wadlin, and Dave Shannon.

Thanks to the participants in my consultation group whose passion in working with couples equal my own: Jill Twohig, Chris Sanderson, Bianca Betz-in, Stacey Mastramatteo, Emily Kahn-Freeman, and Tany Cherkerzian.

Thanks to Carla Sandoval for all her stunning work making sure the world gets to know me via social media and other digital venues, and to Mark Pate for advice and brilliant design work.

I am especially thankful to Jeannette de Beauvoir, friend, editor, and wordsmith who kept pushing me to write this workbook for the world to enjoy.

www.ingramcontent.com/pod-product-compliance
Lightning Source LLC
Chambersburg PA
CBHW061802120626
46550CB00005B/2098